Psalms 51-100

50 Daily Insights by **Mike Raiter**

Journey Through Psalms 51-100
© 2021 by Michael David Raiter
All rights reserved.

Our Daily Bread Publishing is affiliated
with Our Daily Bread Ministries.

Requests for permission to quote
from this book should be directed to:

Permissions Department
Our Daily Bread Publishing
P. O. Box 3566
Grand Rapids, MI 49501, USA

Or contact us by email at
permissionsdept@odb.org

All websites listed are accurate at the time of publication, but may change in the
future or cease to exist. The listing of the website references does not imply our
endorsement of the site's entire contents.

Design by Joshua Tan
Typeset by Haw Shing Yee

ISBN 978-1-913135-46-1

Printed in the United Kingdom
21 22 23 24 25 / 5 4 3 2 1

Foreword

Christians have always loved the book of Psalms. Here are four reasons why.

Psalms gives us the songbook we need to praise God. Written to be sung, the psalms extol God: our Creator, Saviour, and Protector. Music and songs have been a part of every culture in every age, and the psalms give us something worth singing about.

Second, Psalms describes real life. Life can be wonderful with much to thank God for, yet it can be difficult and painful, too. Sometimes Christians pretend that life is good all the time. We don't want to confess that we have doubts or are not coping well. But many psalms are brutally honest about how trying life can be and how difficult it is to keep trusting God. When we have deep feelings, either of joy or sorrow, the psalms give us a song to express these emotions and experiences.

Third, Psalms points us to the Lord Jesus. The New Testament writers looked to the Psalms more than any other Old Testament book to learn about Jesus. They often quoted from the Psalms in their writings. Jesus taught His disciples that the Psalms, like the rest of the Old Testament, spoke about Him (Luke 24:44).

Fourth, the Psalms are like a library of wonderful Christian truths. Psalms teaches us about God, salvation, hope, suffering, sin and obedience, the life of faith, the forces of darkness, and many other truths central to the Christian life.

As you journey through Psalms 51–100, rejoice, weep, and above all, worship our great God and King.

To God be the Glory,
Mike Raiter

We're glad you've decided to join us on a journey into a deeper relationship with Jesus Christ!

For over 50 years, we have been known for our daily Bible reading notes, *Our Daily Bread*. Many readers enjoy the pithy, inspiring, and relevant articles that point them to God and the wisdom and promises of His unchanging Word.

Building on the foundation of *Our Daily Bread*, we have developed the *Journey Through* series to help believers spend time with God in His Word, book by book. We trust this daily meditation on God's Word will draw you into a closer relationship with Him through our Lord and Saviour, Jesus Christ.

How to use this resource

READ: This book is designed to be read alongside God's Word as you journey with Him. It offers explanatory notes to help you understand the Scriptures in fresh ways.

REFLECT: The questions are designed to help you respond to God and His Word, letting Him change you from the inside out.

RECORD: The space provided allows you to keep a diary of your journey as you record your thoughts and jot down your responses.

An Overview

A psalm is, literally, "a song of praise". Therefore, we may assume that the psalms are songs that dwell on all the wonderful things about God and what He has done for us. But these songs also deal with joy and sorrow, blessing and judgement, confidence and doubt. While every psalm will end on a note of trust in God (except Psalm 88), the Psalms collectively express the ups and downs in the life of faith.

Many of the psalms are ascribed to an author and, sometimes, allude to the historical circumstance that gave rise to the psalm. For example, David's adultery led him to compose his psalm of repentance (Psalm 51). David wrote almost half of the psalms (73 to be precise). Other writers were the Sons of Korah, Asaph and his sons, Heman, Solomon, Moses, and Ethan.

There are different kinds of psalms. There are psalms of thanksgiving (e.g. Psalm 98) and psalms of lament (e.g. Psalm 60). There are psalms that express trust in God's goodness (e.g. Psalm 84) and psalms of remembrance, which recall how God saved His people in the past (e.g. Psalm 77). There are wisdom psalms, which contrast two ways of living and the consequences that follow from the choices we make (e.g. Psalm 94). And finally, there are psalms that celebrate Israel's King, who is God's Son, the Anointed One or Messiah (e.g. Psalm 69).

Psalms will do two things for us. First, they teach and admonish us in our walk of faith, encouraging and challenging us (see Colossians 3:16). Second, they give us glorious truths to sing about and "shout for joy to the LORD" (Psalm 100:1).

Key Verse ─────────────────────────────────
Let all creation rejoice before the LORD, for he comes, he comes to judge the earth. He will judge the world in righteousness and the peoples in his faithfulness. —Psalm 96:13

Day 1

Read Psalm 51

Sin has consequences. Few people understood it as well as King David. David's adultery with Bathsheba and his plot to kill her husband, Uriah, marked a turning point in his reign as king of Israel (see 2 Samuel 11–12). In the following chapters of 2 Samuel, we read of the rape of his daughter, Tamar, by David's son Amnon (chapter 13), and then the rebellion of another son, Absalom (chapters 14–19). Rebellion and war plagued the rest of David's reign. David's sin had consequences for his family and the whole nation. But the most serious consequence was how it affected his relationship with God. Fortunately, David confessed his sin after God used Nathan the prophet to confront him.

Psalm 51 is a wonderful model of a sinner's prayer. First, we hear David's confession (vv. 1–6). David understands that he can give God no reason why he should be forgiven. **Forgiveness can only spring from God's grace, "according to your great compassion" (v. 1).** David piles up words to describe the horror of what he has done, "transgressions", "iniquity", "sin", and "evil" (vv. 2–4).

Today, we often describe our sins as "mistakes" or "an error of judgment". David will not play this kind of word game with God to lessen the seriousness of his sin. He admits his sin and that God is right to judge him (v. 4). Finally, David admits that when he sinned, he was acting consistently with his sinful nature (v. 5).

Second, we hear David's desires. David longs to be washed and made clean (vv. 2, 7). He wants his guilt and sin taken away. More than that, he longs for a new heart (v. 10). He wants a heart that desires righteousness, not wickedness. Then "the joy of your salvation" will be restored to him (v. 12).

Finally, David promises to tell the world about all that God has done for him. He will teach other sinners God's ways, so they won't make the same mistakes he made (v. 13). Having experienced the wonder and joy of forgiveness, he will praise God in the presence of all the people (vv. 14–15).

Today, let us thank God for the wonderful gift of His Son, who died that we might be forgiven and begin every day thoroughly cleansed. And as we think about this wonderful psalm, let's also take a moment to confess our sins before God:

> *Almighty God, heavenly Father, we confess that we have failed You often in our thoughts,*

Why does David confess to God, "against you, you only, have I sinned" (Psalm 51:4) when he's sinned against Uriah and his family? Compare Psalm 51:4 with Luke 15:18.

Are there particular sins that you've been hiding from God right now? How does this psalm teach us a right way to confess our sins?

words, and deeds. Not only have we done wrong, but we have failed to do right. Lord, You alone can forgive sin. Because Jesus has died for us, have mercy on us and pardon our sins. Help us to serve You not only with our lips, but with our lives. Amen.

Day 2

Read Psalm 52

1 Samuel 19–31 tells of David's flight from a jealous and murderous King Saul. On one occasion, David came to the godly priest, Ahimelek, who gave him and his supporters consecrated bread and Goliath's sword (1 Samuel 21). The incident was witnessed by Saul's servant, Doeg. Doeg later betrayed Ahimelek to the king and then volunteered to become Saul's executioner. In one of the most brutal acts in the whole Old Testament, Doeg slaughtered all 85 priests of Ahimelek's home town and all the men, women, children and animals in the city (22:16–19).

David remembers Doeg's despicable act of treachery and violence in Psalm 52. This psalm has three parts. The first part recalls Doeg's deceitfulness (Psalm 52:1–4). David emphasises his treachery, "you practise deceit, your tongue plots destruction" (v. 2) and, "you love every harmful word, you deceitful tongue" (v. 4). David describes Doeg's tongue is "like a sharpened razor" (v. 3). It cuts, wounds, and kills. We've all experienced the painful cuts of someone's words. Some of the deepest hurts we experience are the lies and betrayals of people whom we thought we could trust.

In the second part of the psalm (vv. 5–7), David rejoices that God will bring justice and retribution on Doeg. He will come to "everlasting ruin" (v. 5). The Old Testament does not say much about the afterlife, but David clearly believed in judgement and life after death. He knew that death would be an insufficient punishment for Doeg's evil deeds. His ruin deserves to be forever.

In the final section (vv. 8–9), David contrasts his future with Doeg's. While Doeg will be uprooted from the land of the living (v. 5), David will be a flourishing olive tree (v. 8). David described himself as being "in the house of God", even though, whilst on the run, he was far away from God's physical tabernacle in Shiloh. But David understood, as we Christians do, that we remain in God's presence wherever we are.

It's hard to live in a world where people do unspeakable evil, especially when we see them get away with it. The books of Samuel don't tell us what happened to Doeg. It seems he got away with his crimes—in this life. But not in the life to come. **The God who hates evil and loves justice will one day repay people for the evil they have done.** This should encourage us. Although we grieve at the evil around us and sometimes, like David, even feel

When we hear of people doing terrible things to others, especially people we know, how should we respond? What emotions does David express in this psalm? What biblical truths does he hang on to?

Why will the righteous "see and fear" when God brings the wicked to judgment (Psalm 52:6)?

partly responsible (see 1 Samuel 22:20–22), we can rejoice in God's unfailing love towards us. We can be confident that now and always we'll praise Him in the presence of His faithful people (Psalm 52:9).

Day 3

Read Psalm 53

P salm 53 (which largely repeats Psalm 14) is a description of the man or woman who foolishly tries to live without God.

I'm sure that the placement of this psalm after Psalm 52 is deliberate. Doeg was a wicked man who killed God's faithful people because his heart was corrupt and he had no fear of God. He is an example of the "fool" that David describes in Psalm 53.

By his actions, Doeg showed he didn't believe in God. But he probably would have said he did. The people of the ancient world weren't atheists. Many people intellectually affirm there is a God, but this belief doesn't express itself in how they live. Their lives actually proclaim, "there is no God" (Psalm 53:1). This is the kind of person Psalm 53 is describing. **True belief in God is expressed in a life of obedience.**

Psalm 53 describes three features of the fool who denies God. First, their deeds are corrupt (vv. 1–3). Apostle Paul quotes this psalm in his letter to the Romans (see Romans 3:10–12). He gives many examples of this kind of corruption: their lives are full of envy, murder, strife, deceit, malice, and they are gossips, slanderers, God haters, insolent, arrogant, and boastful (Romans 1:28–32). It's not a pretty picture of the character of human beings but it's an accurate diagnosis of a universal condition, "there is no one who does good" (Psalm 53:1).

Second, such people, "devour my people as though eating bread" (v. 4). We saw this in Doeg's slaughter of God's priests. We saw it also in the wickedness of the Jewish leaders who killed Jesus, and later persecuted His followers. We've seen it throughout history as God's people have consistently been persecuted and "devoured" because of their love for the Lord Jesus.

The third feature of the fool is that they "never call on God" (v. 4). They saw no need for God in their life and never cried out to Him. But a day of terror is coming for the fool (v. 5). While alive, they thought they had nothing to fear about God, even though He sees all that they do. One day, though, they'll meet God and realise their folly. But then it will be too late.

Like Psalm 52, this psalm ends with the hope of God bringing salvation from Israel. The Hebrew word for "salvation" is *Yeshua* or Joshua or Jesus. The ultimate hope of ancient Israel is our hope, the true Saviour and King, Jesus.

Psalm 53 is really a loving warning to all the practical atheists in the world. Stop ignoring God. Become wise and turn to Jesus "who rescues us from the coming wrath" (1 Thessalonians 1:10).

ThinkThrough

Can you see some parts of your life where you are living as a "practical atheist", that is, you live as if there were no God?

David says that no one seeks God (Psalm 53:3). However, many people embark on spiritual quests. What are the marks of a genuine search for God?

Day 4

Read Psalm 54

People select names for their children based on a variety of reasons. Some choose names of family members to honour or remember their cherished elders. Some choose names of famous people or Bible characters they admire. Others simply like how the names sound.

The Bible tells us that the Lord's name is shorthand for His character. There's nothing magical in saying the words "Yahweh" or "Jesus", but these names remind us of who God is and what He has done for us. David is surrounded by enemies, but his hope is that God will save him, "by your name . . . by your *might*" (Psalm 54:1). **God's name reminds David of God's saving power that has protected him in all his trials.**

As we saw with Psalm 52, a number of David's psalms were written while he was on the run from the insanely jealous King Saul. As he fled, David found both friends and enemies. This psalm exposes the treachery of the people who lived in the hills of the Desert of Ziph, southeast of Hebron. David was hiding there, but the Ziphites went to Saul to reveal David's hiding place (1 Samuel 23:14–25).

David does three things in this psalm. Each one is an example of how we should respond to trouble. First, he goes straight to God and tells Him the problem (Psalm 54:2–3). It's a good principle for us to follow, too, because God cares for us and has the ability to save. Tell God before anyone else when you're hurt, or in pain or trouble. Look to Him for compassion, mercy, consolation, understanding, and relief. Then we're acknowledging that God, before anyone else, is the one who knows our needs and knows what's best for us.

Second, David affirms his trust in God (vv. 4–5). God had promised him the throne (1 Samuel 16:12–13), so he knew that God would protect him. Mind you, that didn't mean David was complacent. 1 Samuel 23:25 tells us that when he found out that Saul was hunting for him, "he went down to the rock and stayed in the Desert of Maon". David didn't presume upon God's protection; he sought to hide in a safe place, too.

Third, David is confident God will hear his prayer. In fact, he's so sure of God's faithfulness that he sings, "I *will* sacrifice . . . I *will* praise your name" (Psalm 54:6). We may never find ourselves on the run from those who want to kill us, but we may face troubles that seem to overwhelm us, and we may feel like giving up on the Christian race. May we, like David, confidently sing of the Lord's deliverance as if it has already happened (v. 7).

In Philippians 2:9–11, Paul tells us that God has given to Jesus, "the name that is above every name" (v. 9). This is God's own name, the name "Lord". This is the name that David trusted in. This is the name that tells us that Jesus is the loving, just, all-powerful Saviour God. In times of trouble, the Lord Jesus Christ is the name we can trust in; it is the name that should be on our lips.

How has God sustained you through difficult times in your life (Psalm 54:4)?

"I will praise your name, LORD, for it is good" (Psalm 54:6). What does it mean to praise God's name? Why is it good to praise God?

Day 5

Read Psalm 55

1 Peter 5:7 encourages us, "Cast all your anxiety on him because he cares for you". While God embraces *all* our problems, it doesn't mean we would be trouble-free. The letter of 1 Peter is addressed to churches that are suffering persecution, and Peter wrote the letter to encourage believers to keep their faith in Christ and maintain integrity in life (1 Peter 3:13–17).

Persecution is probably the main anxiety that Peter has in mind when he wrote, "your enemy the devil prowls around like a roaring lion looking for someone to devour" (5:8). For how does the devil attack and "devour" Christians? Normally, he works through our human enemies.

It is likely that Psalm 55 is behind 1 Peter 5:7–8. David wrote this psalm when he was surrounded by "destructive forces" (Psalm 55:11). Like the devil, "day and night they prowl about" (v. 10). But David writes at the end of the psalm, "Cast your cares on the LORD and he will sustain you" (v. 22).

Psalm 55 begins with David pouring out his heart to God. He bewails, "my heart is in anguish within me" (v. 4). He longs to be like a dove and fly away from his enemies, "and be at rest" (v. 6). Doves often make their nests in the cleft of a cliff, high above the ground. There they are safe from their predators.

Jesus warned us that we'll be persecuted (see Matthew 10:16–23). Hence, we shouldn't be surprised when enemies of Christ attack us. However, we would be surprised and deeply hurt when someone who claims to be a Christian brother or sister turns against us. Someone you worshipped alongside on Sunday, now plots your ruin on Monday. That was David's situation. He writes, "But it is you . . . my close friend, with whom I once enjoyed sweet fellowship" (Psalm 55:13–14). We don't know who David is referring to. Some think it may have been Ahithophel, David's counsellor, who then joined David's son, Absalom, in rebellion against him (see 2 Samuel 15:12).

What do we do when enemies unjustly attack us? David and Peter speak with one voice. David turns to the Lord for help. He doesn't take up the sword himself. Although David was an accomplished fighter, he trusted God to bring justice. He believed that one day God, "will bring down the wicked into the pit of decay" (Psalm 55:23). Similarly, Peter encouraged his churches, "Do not repay evil with evil or insult with insult" (1 Peter 3:9).

If you've ever experienced injustice then you can identify with David. He's in constant distress and wants to run away. David might have been God's chosen king, but he was just as human as you and me. **David's trust in God didn't take away all his pain, but he knew that the Lord would sustain him. God would help him maintain his integrity.** We can have the same confidence when we cast our anxieties upon Him.

What is troubling you right now? Cast your anxieties on the God who knows, loves, and will sustain you.

The closer the relationship, the deeper the pain of betrayal. How does this psalm help us process our pain in a God-honouring way?

Day 6

Read Psalm 56

What is faith? Having faith is often compared to sitting on a chair: when we sit, we have faith that the chair will hold our weight and not collapse. The problem with this analogy is that a chair is impersonal. It has not made any promises to you that it will hold you up. In contrast, faith that the Bible refers to is personal. It is having trust in *someone,* not *something.* For example, we trust people and what they say to us, even though they let us down sometimes. But God can always be trusted because His word is true. Trusting God is the wonderful refrain in Psalm 56 (vv. 3–4 and 10–11).

The superscription above the psalm reads, "To the tune of 'A Dove on Distant Oaks'". This tells us that David wrote these songs for everyone to sing in the gathered assembly. While the situation he described was particular to his own life, each of God's people can sing the song and apply the words to their own situation.

David had a particular event in mind when he wrote this psalm. 1 Samuel 21:10–15 tells of the time when David sought refuge from Saul in Gath, a Philistine city. Given that David was their sworn enemy, this was a brave and risky thing to do. So "he feigned insanity" and "acted like a madman" (v. 13) while hiding in Gath. Despite this ruse, David sensed the hostility of the city. These people are probably the enemies he describes here in Psalm 56.

The psalm can be divided into two parts. In verses 1–8, David laments his situation and asks for deliverance. His enemies are scheming relentlessly, "hoping to take my life" (Psalm 56:6). We are reminded of the Jewish leaders who, from the early days in Jesus' ministry, conspired together "how they might kill Jesus" (Mark 3:6). David asks God to "list my tears in your scroll" (Psalm 56:8). With this beautiful picture, David asks God to remember all the sufferings he has endured because of his faithfulness. This recording of David's unjust treatment also provides a basis for the Lord's judgment on those who've made him suffer (v. 9). It's a wonderful comfort to know that God both sees and remembers the sufferings of His people.

In the second part of the psalm (vv. 9–13), David expresses his confidence that God will answer his prayer. David had experienced God's deliverance in the past and, more importantly, God had promised him the kingdom. Of course, at this point in David's life, it didn't look like he'd be king one day. He was surrounded by enemies. But **David trusted God's word. This is faith. God** has spoken. We believe that His word is true and He will bring it to fulfilment in our life.

ThinkThrough

When people hear the word "faith", what do they think it means?

How would you explain the meaning of "trusting God" to someone who isn't a Christian?

Day 7

Read Psalm 57

Singing is good for us. A few years ago, I co-authored a book, *Songs of the Saints*, on congregational singing. In the book, we spoke about the power of singing. One reason singing can have such a positive effect on us is that it embraces our emotions as well as our minds. There's now an entire school of psychotherapy called "singing therapy" because people have discovered that through singing, suppressed emotions can thaw out and people can begin to release their inner pain. Psychologist Dr Gene Cohen claimed that tests have shown that elderly people who sing have fewer medical appointments, use less medication, and become less depressed.

It's not surprising, then, that in some of the darkest periods of his life, David writes and sings songs. **David's songs express the pain and injustice of his sufferings, and renew his confidence in the Lord who protects and delivers him at the same time.**

Psalms 52 to 59 mainly recall the time in David's life when King Saul was trying to kill him. The superscription of Psalm 57 tells us that it was written "when he had fled from Saul into the cave". The superscription also tells the song leaders to sing the song to the tune of "Do not Destroy" (see also Psalms 58 and 59). This tune is appropriate given the historical context. 1 Samuel 24 recounts the time when Saul entered a cave where David and his men were hiding. Although David could have easily killed the unsuspecting king, he vows that he will not touch the Lord's anointed (1 Samuel 24:12).

David describes his enemies colourfully. He says they are like "lions" and "ravenous beasts" (Psalm 57:4), stalking their prey. They are like hunters who "spread a net for my feet" (v. 6). Traditionally, scholars believed that David was on the run from Saul for about seven years. If this estimation is accurate, we can appreciate how hard it was for David to be constantly on his guard against those who wanted to kill him.

However, the psalm emphasises David's trust in God. He finds refuge "in the shadow of [God's] wings" (v. 1) and he cries out to the God who saves him (vv. 2–3). David closes his psalm with words of praise to God (vv. 9–11). But before he does that, he affirms that his heart is steadfast, and he will "sing and make music" (v. 7). Indeed, it's as he sings that he "awakens the dawn" in his dark heart (v. 8).

David knew how singing God-centred songs can refocus our thoughts. David knew the power of singing to re-energise our faith and spiritual passion. May the songs we sing produce the same joy and trust in God in our lives.

Apart from "praising God", can you think of other reasons why we sing in church?

Are there times in your life when songs you've heard or sung have deeply ministered to you and strengthened your faith in God?

Day 8

Read Psalm 58

Few things make people angrier than injustice. For example, when governments award lucrative contracts on the basis of bribes or when law courts condemn the innocent and give soft sentences to the guilty. On a personal level, we may be aggrieved when someone less qualified is promoted ahead of us.

Romans 13:4 tells us that God has established the governing authorities "as agents of wrath to bring punishment on the wrongdoer". God loves justice (see Isaiah 61:8) and so He has appointed bodies like the government, the law courts, and the police to promote justice in society. Sadly, these authorities often fail in this work. Indeed, the very institutions established to promote justice could themselves be corrupt. Experiencing or observing injustice usually stirs up our emotions.

In Psalm 58, David is emotionally stirred by the injustice he sees, particularly from people in authority. He could be thinking about the many times he has been the victim.

First, the psalm describes the character of these wicked rulers (Psalm 58:1–5). David observes how their corrupt hearts lead to their unjust deeds and rulings (v. 2). Jesus would echo these words many years later, when he explained that our evil deeds like murder, false testimony, and slander stem from a defiled heart (Matthew 15:16–20). Jesus also said that, "For the mouth speaks what the heart is full of" (12:34).

David saw that these wicked people are born sinners, "from the womb they are wayward, spreading lies" (Psalm 58:3). David likens their lies to the venom of a snake (v. 4). If a poisonous snake "has stopped its ears" and will not listen to its charmer, the charmer has no means to stop it from spreading its poison. Through this colourful metaphor, David tells us that the injustice of the wicked is deliberate and insistent, an inevitable expression of their true character.

The second half of the psalm describes the end of the wicked (vv. 6–11). The colourful images come thick and fast as David asks for God to bring His justice to bear on those who practise injustice (vv. 6–8). **Ultimately, the only real solution to injustice is for God to sweep away the wicked (v. 9).**

All over the world, God's people are being persecuted. Many suffer terribly. Often, it's the government, which has been ordained by God to protect His people, that oppress them. But this psalm ends with David rejoicing that a day of justice will come. In the book of Revelation, the saints sing:

> "Hallelujah!
> Salvation and glory and power belong to our
>   God . . .
> He has avenged on her the blood of his
>   servants" (Revelation 19:1–2).

One day we will sing in that choir.

People often accuse God of injustice. They say, "Why does God let this happen?" How can we respond to these kinds of accusations?

Today let's pray for the persecuted church. Ask God to bring justice and deliverance, and to keep them strong in their faith.

Day 9

Read Psalm 59

1 Samuel 19 recalls the first time David had to flee from Saul. Consumed with jealousy, Saul decided to kill David (v. 1). He "sent men to David's house to watch it and to kill him in the morning" (v. 11). However, Michal, David's wife and Saul's daughter, helped David escape by letting him down through a window. In this psalm, David remembers this event and how God rescued him.

Psalm 59 tells us something about David's enemies and something about David's God.

David speaks about two kinds of enemies. First, he cries out about "fierce men who conspire against me" (Psalm 59:3). They are sent by Saul to kill David, whom he sees as a threat to his throne. Second, he implores God "to punish all the nations" (v. 5) who are "snarling like dogs" (v. 6). Though two separate groups of people, they are connected in their desire to kill David. And in opposing God's anointed king, both Saul and the nations are united in opposing God. As such, Saul, his supporters, and the surrounding nations will face God's judgment (vv. 5, 8, 13).

In Ephesians 6:12, Paul tells us that our struggle is not against flesh and blood but against the evil spiritual powers. Of course, Paul knew that his enemies were real people like false teachers and those who persecuted him. But Paul also knew that behind them, working through them, were "the powers of this dark world and . . . the spiritual forces of evil in the heavenly realms". Like David, Paul prayed for deliverance from both these enemies.

Psalm 59 also teaches us about David's God. As David goes through various trials, he continually relies on God's steadfast love. He sings, "in the morning I will sing of your love" (v. 16). David knew that God's love for him was expressed most wonderfully in that He would exalt him and make him the ruler over His people Israel (see 1 Samuel 16). Even under the threat of death, David relies on God's loving commitment to him to keep this promise.

But David wrote this psalm to be sung by all Israel. All Israel could rely on God's steadfast love. God will keep His promise to make them into a great nation that will bring blessing to all the world.

Christians, too, live every day relying on the Lord's steadfast love. As we face our enemies, both personal and spiritual, we rely on the same loving God who keeps His promises to us.

I'm sure there were moments when David wondered whether he'd survive. We, too, might wonder whether we can keep going as faithful disciples from time to time. But, like David, we can share the same confidence in the Lord, "I will sing of your strength; in the morning I will sing of your love" (Psalm 59:16).

In Ephesians 6:11 Paul writes of the "devil's schemes". What do you think are some of the devil's schemes that are intended to undermine your trust in God?

Why does God's destruction of His people's enemies cause everyone to know "that God rules over Jacob" (Psalm 59:13)? How will God's final judgment on His enemies cause people to know that He rules over His church?

Day 10

Read Psalm 60

In life there are successes and failures. Sometimes a new job works out and sometimes it doesn't. Some churches grow and some close. These failures may not have a moral cause. However, at other times failures in our life do have a moral cause. Sometimes we sin and do suffer the consequences.

While the books of Samuel portray David as a successful warrior-king, Israel also knew defeat under his rule. Psalm 60 describes the impact of one such defeat.

The heading of the psalm seems to be at odds with the psalm itself. We're told it's a psalm that celebrates how David and his commander Joab "fought . . . and struck down twelve thousand Edomites". The psalm speaks of David's confidence that the Lord will come to Israel's aid (Psalm 60:11). But when he wrote this song, the battle was yet to be won.

Psalm 60 begins by acknowledging that Israel has suffered defeat in battle. Ultimately, this defeat is not due to Israel fighting a stronger army but to the Lord rejecting them in His anger (v. 1). We're not told what sin Israel has committed, but they are staggering like drunk men who have consumed the wine of God's wrath (v. 3).

David, however, is confident that the Lord will deliver them. God has "raised a banner" (v. 4). In other words, God has shown that He is ready to fight for them. David knows this because God will never abandon "those who fear [Him]" (v. 4).

In vv. 6–8, God himself speaks. God promised the land of Canaan to His people and He will ensure that the tribes keep their inheritance (vv. 6–7). The presence of Israel in the land is a sign that this is God's land and He has power ("Ephraim is my helmet") and authority ("Judah is my sceptre"). Israel's victory will mean the humiliation of her enemies. These godless nations will serve Israel. They'll be little more than a "washbasin" (v. 8), something only useful for washing hands and feet. The picture of the tossing of the sandal (v. 8) is probably just another way of emphasising the complete subjection of these nations to Israel.

In the last verses (vv. 9–12), David affirms his confidence in God. Although it felt as if the Lord had left them, David believes that the Lord will again lead them into victory. Indeed, God has to. If God is not with them, they have no hope. But with the Lord, "we shall gain the victory" (v. 12).

Failure or defeat is never the last word. The hope that Christians have is even greater than the hope of Israel. **Since God has placed all things under the feet of Jesus (Ephesians 1:22), we are confident "the Lord will rescue me from every evil attack and bring me safely to his heavenly kingdom" (2 Timothy 4:18).**

"For human help is worthless" (Psalm 60:11). What do you think David meant by this when we know that God has given us people in the church to help us in times of need?

"[God] will trample down our enemies" (Psalm 60:12). How can we avoid the danger of being over-confident in the Christian life?

Day 11

Read Psalm 61

We live in an unsafe world. My wife and I live in a city apartment. We love our home and the convenience of being at the centre of a vibrant city. But it comes with a cost. In the past six years, we've experienced at least eight break-ins or attempted break-ins. Every day many of us live with physical insecurity. Some of us also face spiritual and emotional insecurity. We may feel under threat from danger, turmoil, or opposition. In such moments, we long for someone who can protect us.

In Psalm 61, David shares his insecurity. He's under threat and doesn't feel safe. Unlike some of the previous psalms, David doesn't explain his particular circumstances. Instead, he speaks generally about a threat that has caused his heart to grow faint (Psalm 61:2). His pain is intense and his prayer is a desperate cry (v. 1).

David needs a place of safety. He uses four colourful images to describe God, the only one in whom he can find safety. First, God is "the rock that is higher than I" (v. 2). God is strong, stable, and reliable, far more than any human being. Second, God is "a strong tower" (v. 3), a place of strength and refuge. Third, David longs to "dwell in [God's] tent for ever" (v. 4). The tent, or tabernacle, was symbolically God's dwelling place. Just like a weary traveller finds rest, refreshment, and protection in someone's tent, so David longs to know the security of being in God's presence. Finally, he wants "to take refuge in the shelter of your wings" (v. 4). This common biblical metaphor (see Psalm 36:7; 57:1; 63:7; 91:4) is a picture of helpless chicks being protected by their mother.

David is confident that God has heard his prayer because He has given to him the promised land (Psalm 61:5). This affirms that God has reserved a wonderful inheritance, which is their salvation, for those who fear Him. David knew his salvation wouldn't be taken away from him.

David's final request is for himself as king. He desires, through his descendants, to reign forever and always be in God's presence (vv. 6–7). Historically, David's earthly kingdom wouldn't last. These words only find their fulfilment in Jesus. The book of Hebrews tells us that, like David, Jesus "offered up prayers and petitions with fervent cries and tears to the one who could save him from death" (Hebrews 5:7). And it is King Jesus who rules forever, "being enthroned in God's presence" (Psalm 61:7).

Who do you turn to when you feel insecure? Like you, Jesus knew tears. But He also knew the rescue of God. **Jesus now rules over all powers, watching over His people. There is no rock higher, mightier, and more reliable than Him. Turn to Him.**

When have you felt unsafe? To whom did you turn to at such times?

How did God protect you in the past? How did you respond to His protection?

Day 12

Read Psalm 62

What does it mean to "rest in God"? "Rest" usually stands in opposition to work. It's doing nothing instead of doing something. It's finding a quiet place for a much-needed sleep. Psalm 62 tells us to "rest in God" (vv. 1, 5). While we are to cease from striving in our own strength, resting in God isn't about taking things easy. True spiritual resting is purposeful and active.

Once again, it is the assaults of his enemies that leads David to turn to God and express his fears and hope through the words of a song. David's cry to God, "How long" (v. 3), suggests he has been suffering for a while and sees no end in sight. His suffering is taking its toll on him. He likens himself to a "leaning wall" and a "tottering fence". Once David felt strong and stood straight, but now the winds of constant opposition have bent and weakened him.

David turns to God, his only fortress and rock (vv. 5–7). There's no point in looking to other people for rescue. All people are nothing but puffs of air, as light as a human breath. They may appear strong and reliable but this appearance is deceptive (v. 9). Of course, the Lord uses people to support and encourage us in times of trouble, but David reminds us that in all difficulties, God should be the first person we go to for help, compassion, and comfort.

Having spoken to God, David now speaks to the congregation. He calls on them to also trust in God (v. 8). **Trusting God expresses itself in living a life that pleases Him.** David warns against accumulating wealth, especially wealth gained illegally (v. 10). Jesus also warned us not to set our hearts on riches (Matthew 6:20–21). Instead, we should "seek first his kingdom and his righteousness" (v. 33), trusting God to provide for us as we serve Him. That's resting in God.

In the final verses, David sums up all he's been saying with two principles. First, remember that God is both powerful and loving (Psalm 62:11–12). Therefore, in any and every situation we can turn to Him for help. The second principle is that God will judge every person for how they have lived (v. 12). If we have trusted and obeyed God like David, we can take comfort in knowing that God will finally punish those who have oppressed His people and lived corrupt lives.

The power and love that God has shown us is ultimately expressed in the gift of His Son, who has rescued us and given us rest. Jesus invites, "Come to me, all you who are weary and burdened, and I will give you rest" (Matthew 11:28). And Jesus says He is coming again. We have the certainty and comfort of a coming day of judgment. These are two great truths we can build our lives upon.

ThinkThrough

What are some things that rob you of your spiritual, physical, and mental rest? Read Psalm 62 again and make a list of the wonderful truths this psalm expresses that can help you find rest.

David encourages us to "pour out your hearts to him" (Psalm 62:8). One way we can do that is through the words of Psalms. Can you think of creative ways in which you can use psalms like Psalm 62 to "pour out your hearts to him"?

Day 13

Read Psalm 63

One of the criticisms I hear about many modern praise songs is that they're too individualistic. We sing to God, "I will love you" or "I will praise you". The critics say that singing is a communal activity so our songs should be more about "we" than "me". Apparently, no one told King David that. While he wrote his songs to be sung by all God's people, he often spoke very personally of his own relationship with God. In Psalm 63, David says, "I", "me", or "my"—no less than 20 times.

In words reminiscent of Psalm 42, David expresses a deep thirst to be in God's presence. This thirst is probably both physical and spiritual. In the title of the psalm, we're told he was in "the Desert of Judah", probably on the run from either Saul or his son Absalom. But he longs to be back in the sanctuary, the symbolic dwelling place of God (Psalm 63:2).

In vv. 3–5 David expresses his deep love for God. When the 2nd century Christian bishop, Polycarp, was facing death before a Roman governor, he was offered his freedom if he denied Christ. Polycarp replied, "For 86 years I have been his servant, and he has never wronged me. How can I blaspheme my king who saved me?" Like David, this bishop knew that God's love was better than life. Indeed, to know God turns our thirst into a feast (v. 5). His love is even richer and more satisfying than our favourite food.

Food and drink are essential for life. It's not surprising, then, that poets and preachers have often chosen them as metaphors to describe our relationship with God. Jesus used the same metaphor, too. After feeding a hungry crowd of 5000 men (plus women and children), John tells us that they, "ate as much as they wanted" (John 6:11). As the bread Jesus gave them satisfied the crowd abundantly, it symbolised the fact that He is the bread of life (v. 35). Jesus was telling them, and us today, that by believing in Him who gave His life for us (v. 51), we will receive true life that will completely satisfy us. Indeed, to know Jesus is better than life.

Next, David shares his thoughts at night. This is usually the time when we feel most vulnerable, as fears and nightmares assail us. But David's thoughts turn to God. He remembers how God has helped him in the past (Psalm 63:6). David is like a small child who, when crossing a busy road, heard his mother says, "hold my hand and you'll be safe". So, when the terrors of night come upon him, David clings to God's right hand of power (v. 8). The song concludes with

David's expression of trust that God will deliver him from his enemies (vv. 9–11).

God richly satisfies those who hunger and thirst for Him.
This is why it's appropriate for us, both as individuals and as the church, to praise Him with singing lips (v. 5).

ThinkThrough

What place should praise and adoration play in our devotional life? How could you incorporate more praise into your times alone with God?

What are the kinds of thirsts that many people suffer? Read John 7:37–39. How does the Lord Jesus satisfy our thirst?

Day 14

Read Psalm 64

True justice is sometimes hard to find. Sometimes the guilty go free, or the innocent end up being punished. Or, even when the guilty is punished, the punishment doesn't fit the crime and is either too severe or too lenient. Of course, perfect justice can only come from the perfect knowledge of a perfect judge. In Psalm 64, David cries out to God for this kind of justice.

The psalm begins with David begging God to "hear me" and "hide me" (Psalm 64:1–2). He is the victim of a conspiracy by some enemies. He's outnumbered by those who want to do him harm. He wants God to hear his cry for help and to protect him.

In vv. 3–6, David tells us three things about his enemies. First, their weapons are words. Though many of us may go through life without ever being the victims of physical violence, few of us will ever escape the pain of verbal violence. People gossip, tell lies, or bring false accusations against us. These "cruel words [are] like deadly arrows" (v. 3). Second, David's enemies are sneaky. "They shoot from ambush . . . hiding their snares" (vv. 4–5). They plot their schemes in secret. Those whom we think are friends suddenly attack us. Third, his enemies are arrogant, thinking they've concocted "a perfect plan" (v. 6).

David knew such schemers, and so did our Lord Jesus. The Gospels describe the repeated plots of the Jewish leaders against Jesus. On a number of occasions, they asked Him questions that appeared genuine but were, in fact, intended "to catch him in his words" (Mark 12:13). Matthew tells us that while Jesus was in Jerusalem, the chief priests, the elders of the people, and the high priest conspired "to arrest Jesus secretly and kill him" (Matthew 26:3–4). Jesus would be convicted on the basis of false testimony and rumour.

What will God do to such people? David tells us that He will treat them justly. To those who fire arrows at God's innocent servant, God will shoot arrows at them. Those who try to suddenly strike down David will now suddenly be struck down by God (Psalm 64:7). God is a God of justice; in the same way that people treat others, God will treat them.

How will people respond to such a just God? How should we respond? Psalm 63 gives us six ways in vv. 9–10. *Fear* **the God who will always judge with perfect justice.** *Proclaim* **His mighty salvation.** *Ponder* **what He has done.** *Rejoice* **in the Lord.**

Take refuge in Him. ***Glory*** in Him. Take some time to do that now.

ThinkThrough

Why are "arrows" such an effective metaphor for words that wound? According to Psalm 64, how can we protect ourselves from such attacks?

"But God will shoot them with his arrows" (Psalm 64:7). What are the "arrows" of God?

_____

_____

_____

_____

_____

_____

_____

_____

_____

_____

_____

_____

_____

_____

_____

_____

_____

_____

Day 15

Read Psalm 65

The 4th century church bishop, Augustine, once said that the Christian should be "a hallelujah from head to foot". He meant that we are, and should be, constantly thanking and praising God for all He has done for us. In Psalm 65, we turn from laments to some songs of thanksgiving.

David describes three displays of God's goodness and power. First, God deserves our praise because He forgives our sins (Psalm 65:3–4). Psalm 51 was a confession of personal sin, but Psalm 65 is a confession of communal sin, "we were overwhelmed by sins" (v. 3). **It's appropriate for individual Christians to confess their sins, but there's also a time for a whole church to acknowledge where they have failed as God's people.** The church in Laodicea was a church whom Jesus invited them to acknowledge their sin ("cover your shameful nakedness") and be in fellowship with Him again (Revelation 3:18, 20). Similarly, in Psalm 65, one of the wonderful results of confession and forgiveness is that God's people again "live in your courts" (v. 4).

Second, God is worthy of praise because "you answer us with awesome and righteous deeds" (v. 5). David may still be thinking of God's awesome power expressed in restoring His sinful people to himself as he reminds us of God's power, which rules and controls the land and sea. Jesus' disciples experienced this personally on the Sea of Galilee when their Master "stilled the roaring of the seas" (v. 7; see also Matthew 8:26). The disciples' response was amazement. Or, in the words of our psalm, "the whole earth is filled with awe at your wonders" (v. 8).

Finally, David thanks God for the abundant harvest He gives to the earth (vv. 9–13). As David writes, he sees streams filled with water, rain from heaven, and meadows filled with flocks. Sometimes famine and scarcity are signs of God's judgment. For instance, three years of famine was one of the options God gave David as punishment for taking an unlawful census (1 Chronicles 21:12). Given this psalm begins with thanksgiving for God's forgiveness, it's quite possible that this earthly abundance is a tangible expression that Israel has been restored to God. While we should not see all "natural" disasters as God's judgment on a particular people for a particular sin, we can always see the earth's bounty and fertility as the expression of God's "awesome and righteous deeds" (Psalm 65:5).

One of my morning prayers is, *I praise and thank You for Your gifts in creation: for this beautiful world, for food and drink, for Your daily provision of life and health, for earth, sky and sea, plants animals, and birds.*

_____

_____

_____

_____

_____

_____

ThinkThrough

Have you had an experience where a group of Christians have needed to come together for corporate repentance and confession? What do we pray at times like this?

Are we in danger of taking God's "natural" gifts for granted? How can we avoid doing this?

_____

_____

_____

_____

_____

_____

_____

_____

_____

_____

_____

Read Psalm 66

Praising God is one of the most important things Christians do. While there are many types of psalms (confession, lament, thanksgiving) the word "psalm" literally means "a song of praise". From beginning to end the Bible rings in praise of God. Numerous books of the Bible contain songs of praise (e.g. Exodus 15; Judges 5; 2 Samuel 22; Isaiah 26; Luke 1:46–55). In Ephesians, apostle Paul says that the purpose of all that God has done for us in Christ is "to the praise of his glorious grace" (Ephesians 1:6). We're given a picture of the fulfilment of this in the songs of praise in Revelation (e.g. Revelation 5:9–14; 7:10–17).

Psalm 66 opens where Psalm 65 ended, " . . . shout for joy and sing" (65:13) and "Shout for joy to God" (66:1). In the first section (vv. 1–12), the psalmist commands everyone to "sing the glory of his name" (v. 2). All the earth will bow down before God (v. 4). Some will bow down gladly because they know personally what God has done for them. Others will bow down reluctantly because they cannot deny that God's deeds are awesome (v. 3; see also Philippians 2:9–11).

When the songwriter thinks of God's awesome deeds, he particularly recalls the rescue from Egypt in the crossing of the Red Sea (v. 6) and God's care and discipline of Israel in the wilderness before they entered the promised land (vv. 9–12).

The psalmist then promises to bring his sacrifices to the God who heard his prayer for deliverance (vv. 13–15). Of course, we don't bring offerings of bulls and goats today. We present our lives as a daily sacrifice to God instead (Romans 12:1).

Why did God answer the songwriter's prayer? Because he didn't cherish sin in his heart (Psalm 66:18). John's Gospel reminds us, "We know that God does not listen to sinners. He listens to the godly person who does his will" (John 9:31). **When we're harbouring sin, we often find it hard to pray. More seriously, the Bible repeatedly warns us that unconfessed sin can be a serious barrier to God answering our prayers** (Job 27:7–9; Proverbs 15:29; 1 John 3:21–22).

In many churches, basic Bible knowledge is lacking. The songs we sing, which often lack biblical content, are partly to blame for this. There are few modern songs of confession or lament. The songs we sing shape the truths we believe. It's important for Christian faith and maturity that we sing songs that will help us to continually know, understand, and be reminded of what Jesus has done for us and the character of the Christian life. In her songs, Israel remembered the time when she was a pilgrim people, enduring hard times in the wilderness on her way to her inheritance in Canaan. Similarly, may the songs we sing remind us of God's awesome deeds of salvation and inspire us to keep moving forward in faith and obedience.

ThinkThrough

What are the reasons the psalmist gives for praising God? When we praise God, what do we praise Him for? How can Psalm 66 instruct us in the way we praise God?

Has unconfessed sin affected your relationship with God? How? What will you do about it?

Read Psalm 67

Psalm 67 is a psalm of praise and thanksgiving that was probably used at harvest festivals. Some churches today still celebrate harvest festivals. People bring gifts of food to the church to distribute to the needy. These gifts are visible reminders of God's grace and generosity towards us. This psalm gives a fresh perspective on how we should view God's blessings.

Psalm 67 is a simple song in three short sections. It is structured like three concentric circles. The outer circle is vv. 1–2, 6–7. The psalm opens and closes with a request for God to bless His people (vv. 1–2, 6–7), and continue to treat them kindly and generously. But why should God bless us? The psalmist adds, "That your ways may be known on earth, your saving power among all nations" (v. 2). We seek God's blessing so that the world will know of His wonder and saving power.

Then there is the inner circle (vv. 3, 5), where the call to praise God is repeated. **When we realise how generously God has physically and spiritually blessed us, the only right response is to praise Him.** One of the greatest sins in our world is that we walk daily by markets full of God's good gifts to us and never give a thought about the One who truly puts all the food on the shelves. It is God who causes the land to yield its harvest (v. 6).

The heart of the psalm is verse 4. The songwriter praises God for His justice and His great plan for the world. We Christians have an even greater reason to praise God for this. Where do we see God's justice and power most wonderfully displayed? In arguably the most important sentence in his letters, Paul wrote, "God presented Christ as a sacrifice of atonement, through the shedding of his blood—to be received by faith. He did this to demonstrate his righteousness . . ." (Romans 3:25).

God watches people walk the aisles of shops that are overflowing with everything that one could possibly ever want and need. Everything is ultimately from His generous hand. He is their Creator, Provider, and Redeemer. Yet, very few stop to praise Him. But God did not punish people for their ingratitude. Instead He sent His Son to die on the cross so they could be forgiven. The cross is the place where mercy and justice meet. That's why the nations will sing for joy.

Many nations are poor. Some are materially poor. But all are spiritually poor. God longs to bless the nations by showing them His justice and power. God can and will do that through us. We've been blessed to be a blessing to others. That's the message of Psalm 67.

ThinkThrough

How do you and your church celebrate the wonderful generosity of God towards us?

Think of those in need around you. How can you use God's blessings upon you to be a blessing to them?

Day 18

Read Psalm 68

Who is our God? He is our King, Saviour, Father, and Shepherd. He is also our Warrior. Throughout the Bible, God is described as the One who victoriously leads His armies, both heavenly and earthly, into battle for the sake of His weak and defenceless people whom He loves (e.g. Exodus 15:3; 1 Samuel 17:45; Isaiah 42:13). We meet this Warrior God in Psalm 68.

The psalm begins with David remembering Israel's march to the promised land. The book of Numbers records the events that David refers to. It begins with a census of all the men eligible to fight in Israel's army as they enter Canaan. Whenever they set out on their military marches, Moses would say, "Rise up, LORD, may your enemies be scattered; may your foes flee before you" (Numbers 10:35). David recalls these words as he asks God for victory over his enemies (Psalm 68:1). The Warrior God is also the one who "rides on the clouds" and "across the highest heavens" (vv. 4, 33; see also Deuteronomy 33:26; Isaiah 19:1; Nahum 1:3). It's a picture of God leading His army across the heavens to save His people, a theme that runs throughout the psalm (Psalm 68:1–2, 14, 18, 20, 23, 30–31).

This Warrior God fights for His helpless people, the fatherless, the widows, the lonely, and the prisoners (vv. 5–6). On the one hand, these descriptions refer to the actual physical condition of the poor and needy in the society. In the ancient patriarchal society, the fatherless and widows have limited means to meet their financial needs. On the other hand, they are also pictures of a human being's spiritual condition. Jesus used similar metaphors to describe His people—they are the poor in spirit (Matthew 5:3) and they are the hungry and thirsty for righteousness (v. 6). He described His ministry as coming to proclaim good news to the poor and to set the prisoners free (Luke 4:18).

Apostle Paul quotes Psalm 68:18 when he writes to the church in Ephesus (Ephesians 4:8). He sees this psalm as a picture of Christ's victory for us and encouraged the Christians repeatedly to remember the mighty power of God available to them (1:19; 3:20–21; 6:10) in their struggle against "the powers of this dark world and against the spiritual forces of evil in the heavenly realms" (6:12).

Indeed, there are so many similarities between Ephesians and Psalm 68 that one New Testament scholar, Clinton Arnold, suggests that, "the entirety of this psalm may have been on Paul's mind as he penned Ephesians".[1] Similarly, Tremper Longman III writes, that "by the New

Testament period Psalm 68 was read and applied to the work of Christ both in His first coming when He defeated Satan on the cross as well as His second coming when He will accomplish a final victory over all evil people and spiritual powers".[2]

Psalm 68 ends on this note, "the God of Israel gives power and strength to his people" (Psalm 68:35). **Christians have even greater reasons to sing and "proclaim the power of God" (v. 34) because Christ has come and He is coming again!**

[1] Clinton E. Arnold, *Exegetical Commentary on the New Testament: Ephesians* (Zondervan, 2010), 248

[2] Tremper Longman III, *Psalms* (IVP, 2014), 261

In your Christian life when do you feel weak and helpless? How can the truths of this psalm encourage you?

Reflect on the images of the fatherless, widow, lonely, and prisoner. What do these pictures express about the Christian life?

Day 19

Read Psalm 69

I regularly thank God for family and friends. These are people who love me and to whom I can turn in times of need. But imagine having no one to turn to in your distress. How would you feel? Where would you go if everyone who once supported you now rejected you? The only person you can turn to is God. That is what David expresses in Psalm 69.

Why is David suffering? Once again, we are not given the details of David's situation. This is deliberate because the psalms have been written and collated to provide a model for believers on how to relate with God.

How is David feeling? He is overwhelmed. He feels like a man who is drowning and can barely keep his head above water. His troubles are like "floods that engulf me" (Psalm 69:2; see also vv. 14–15).

What does David do? David brings his complaint to God. There are two parts to his complaint. First, he has been hated "without reason" (v. 4) and "endured scorn for [God's] sake" (v. 7; see also vv. 19–20). **Throughout history, the church has faced intense persecution for no other reason than her devotion to Jesus.** Similarly, in schools, universities, and workplaces across the world today, Christians face prejudice and abuse simply because they love the Lord Jesus.

The second part of his complaint is that he has been rejected by those closest to him (vv. 8, 20). He turned to people who were his friends for support, but received mockery instead. David parallels this to asking for food and drink, but being given "gall" and "vinegar" (v. 21). Gall is a kind of poison; vinegar intensifies your thirst rather than quench it.

Faced with abuse from enemies and cold-hearted rejection by friends and family, it's not surprising that David is "worn out calling for help" (v. 3). He is emotionally exhausted. David pled with the Lord to "answer me quickly" (v. 17).

Psalm 69 tells the story of a righteous man unjustly persecuted and rejected by the people he loved. It's not surprising that this is one of the most oft-quoted psalms in the New Testament because it points forward to Christ:

- Jesus quoted verse 4 when He spoke about the hatred the world has towards himself and His disciples (John 15:18–25).
- John quoted verse 9 to show that Jesus fulfilled the verse when He cleansed the temple (John 2:17).

- Luke quoted verse 25 to show that the apostles saw the death of Judas as fulfilment of that verse (Acts 1:20).

- Paul applied verses 22–23 to Jews who hardened their hearts and didn't respond to God through Jesus (Romans 11:9–10).

- Paul quoted verse 9 to encourage us to follow the example of Jesus who pleased others and not himself (Romans 15:3).

Can you think of times in your life when you felt like you were drowning and overwhelmed by troubles? How can Psalm 69 provide you with a model for prayer at such a time?

Many people suffer the rejection of their family because of their faith in Christ. How can we support brothers and sisters in this situation?

Read Psalm 70

One aspect of the fruit of the Spirit is patience. I confess that I don't do well in that department. I'm impatient when I'm stuck in traffic or in a queue, or when I'm kept waiting on the line until an operator is available to take my call. I doubt that I'm the only person who feels this way. We want instant answers and instant satisfaction. In Psalm 70, David has grown tired of waiting.

Psalm 70 is a song of lament. Sandwiched between two long laments (Psalms 69 and 71), this short psalm is almost identical to Psalm 40:13–17. The psalm begins and ends with a plea by David for God to hurry. He prays, "Hasten, O God to save me; come quickly . . . do not delay" (70:1, 5).

David's situation in this psalm seems similar to Psalm 69. He is being attacked by enemies who want to kill him (v. 2; see 69:4). He is the object of their scorn and mockery (v. 3; see 69:10, 12, 19–20).

David's prayer is for justice (vv. 2–3). He wants God to treat his enemies in the same way that they have treated him. It's good to pray for justice and we are assured that one day God "will repay each person according to what they have done" (Romans 2:6).

But let's not forget that God has not treated us as we have deserved. When we were His enemies, He saved us by His grace (Ephesians 2:5). The Lord Jesus when facing mockery on the cross, prayed that His enemies might be forgiven (Luke 23:34). We should emulate the Lord's example. Before seeking justice, we should first of all pray like this, "Lord, as You were merciful to us, when we were Your enemies, please show mercy to those who oppress us."

Christians are a group of people who are waiting for justice. Jesus warned us that we would have to endure suffering and persecution (see Mark 10:29–30) and that has been the experience of many believers. At such times, we echo the last prayer recorded in the Bible, "Amen, come Lord Jesus" (Revelation 22:20). **It has been a long wait, as the Lord Jesus told us (Matthew 25:5, 19), but He *will* come and save us and bring justice.** In the meantime, we must be patient and, like David, keep praying, "LORD, do not delay" (v. 5). Then we who long for God's saving help will always say, "The LORD is great" (v. 4).

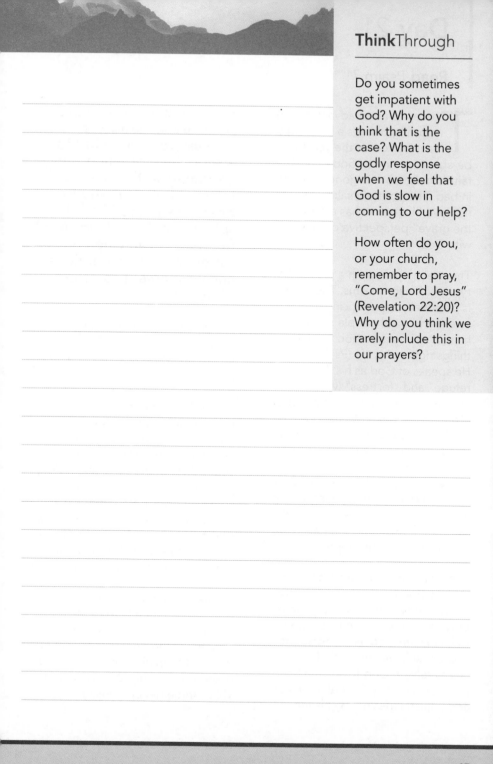

Do you sometimes get impatient with God? Why do you think that is the case? What is the godly response when we feel that God is slow in coming to our help?

How often do you, or your church, remember to pray, "Come, Lord Jesus" (Revelation 22:20)? Why do you think we rarely include this in our prayers?

Day 21

Read Psalm 71

There are many advantages in growing old. It's a blessing to look back over the years and be able to testify to God's consistent faithfulness, both in good times and in bad. The poet of Psalm 71 (we're not given his name) has a "cradle to the grave" perspective on walking with God.

The psalm opens with a prayer that is typical of many psalms. The psalmist is personally experiencing injustice, as evil and cruel people are attacking him, so he looks to God to make things right in his life (Psalm 70:4). He speaks of God as his "rock of refuge" and "fortress" (v. 3), again familiar pictures of God as our strong protector. Repeatedly, he looks to God's righteousness or His "righteous deeds" as his hope for deliverance (vv. 2, 15–16, 19, 24). Since God is righteous, the psalmist is confident that He will make everything wrong in the world right. This means both salvation for him and shame, scorn, and disgrace for his oppressors (v. 13).

The psalmist confesses his lifelong trust in God (vv. 5–9). Since birth, he has been faithful to God. He now prays for the strength to continue walking with God as he gets older and weaker. He knows that he has to rely on God to sustain him, particularly in the face of intense and unjust suffering. By his life of consistent faithfulness, he has "become a sign to many" (v. 7).

It's easy to praise God for a short time or when things are going well. However, to see a believer who has been "declaring [God's] splendour all day long" (v. 8) for years, even when he is suffering, is a tremendous encouragement to other Christians.

The psalmist continues to reflect on his life in verses 14–18. Praising God for His righteous acts has been the poet's practice, "since my youth . . . to this day . . . when I am old and grey" (vv. 17–18). Sometimes Christians might wonder what they can do when they retire or grow old. Psalm 71 gives us a wonderful calling: to "declare your power to the next generation, your mighty acts to all who are to come" (v. 18). These mighty acts would be both God's great work of salvation for us, achieved by Christ's death and resurrection, and our personal stories of God's care for us.

A parent's first and foremost job is to pass on their faith to their children. The apostle Paul reminds Timothy of the sincere faith that he received from his mother, Eunice and grandmother, Lois (2 Timothy 1:5). That's three generations of faithfulness! May the Lord use us to pass on the faith to the next generation, too.

ThinkThrough

Can you think of older, godly saints who have inspired you in your Christian walk? How have they been a good example to you?

What are some ways that you can declare God's power to the next generation?

Day 22

Read Psalm 72

The Bible tells us that we should pray for our government (1 Timothy 2:1–2). What do you look for in a good government? We want a government that brings peace and prosperity. We want a government that is just and cares for the weakest and most vulnerable in our society. If God were to give us such a government, we would want them to stay in power for a long time.

Psalm 72, the final poem of Book 2* of Psalms, describes an ideal ruler. As the only psalm attributed to Solomon, it fittingly reflects its writer's wisdom. In the opening two verses, Solomon asks God to endow the king with justice and righteousness so that he will always make good and right decisions, particularly for "the afflicted ones" (v. 2).

These verses lay the foundation for the rest of the psalm, which goes on to describe four features of God's ideal king.

First, he will bring prosperity to his people (vv. 3, 7, 16). The word translated "prosperity" is the Hebrew word, *shalom*. It can also mean "peace" or "harmony". Under this king's rule, the people will enjoy material, social, political, and spiritual blessings.

Second, this king will be especially caring towards the poor and needy. He will deliver them from their many troubles (vv. 2, 4, 12–14). Those who are weak are easily abused and exploited. God's good king will protect them and ensure they receive justice.

Third, this king will bring blessing to all the world (vv. 8–11, 16–17). Under his rule, Israel's power and influence will grow, and the kings of the world will bring him gifts (v. 15). This was fulfilled when the wise men from the east visited Jesus to bring him gifts of gold, frankincense and myrrh (Matthew 2:1–11). God's great promise to Abraham was that, as God blessed Abraham's family then, "all peoples on earth will be blessed through you" (Genesis 12:1–3). This faithful king would be the fulfilment of that promise.

Finally, such a king will reign forever (Psalm 72:5, 15).

For a short while, it may have seemed that God answered the prayer of this psalm in King Solomon. But it soon became clear that he fell far short of this ideal. While he began well, as he grew older, he became an oppressor of his people (1 Kings 12:4) and his heart was not fully devoted to the Lord (11:4). Faithful Jews continued to look forward to the coming of the godly king of Psalm 72. All the promises of this psalm finally found their fulfilment in the coming of the Lord Jesus. **Jesus is the just and righteous king through whom all nations are blessed** (Galatians 3:7–8; Revelation 7:9–10).

We are the servants of King Jesus. He calls us the salt of the earth. It is through us that God spreads *shalom*, cares for the poor, and brings salvation to all people.

* Psalms contains five books. Book 1 is Psalms 1–41, Book 2 is Psalms 42–72, Book 3 is Psalms 73–89, Book 4 is Psalms 90–106, and Book 5 is Psalms 107–150.

ThinkThrough

Is it right to expect our governments to reflect the features of the ideal ruler as described in Psalm 72? Why or why not?

How should we care for the poor and needy? Should we be seeking our nation's prosperity and, if so, how?

Read Psalm 73

The oldest moral dilemma is, "Why do bad things happen to good people?" or "Why do good things happen to bad people?" We'd like our world to be fairer. We'd like God to treat people as they deserve, where good people live a long and happy life, and evil people pay for their crimes in this lifetime. Sadly, life isn't like that. This problem almost caused the writer of Psalm 73 to give up his faith.

While Book 2 ended on a high note of joy and optimism for God's good king, Book 3 begins with doubt and confusion. The first 11 psalms in Book 3 are written by the Levite musician, Asaph (see 1 Chronicles 15:17–19).

Psalm 73:1 affirms a great biblical truth: God is good to the pure in heart. Jesus called them "blessed" (Matthew 5:8). Quickly, though, the poet shares what almost made him lose his foothold and caused him to wander away from the faith (Psalm 73:2). He observed that the wicked enjoy the easy life. They are healthy and strong, and almost seem immune from the normal troubles of life. They are arrogant and give no thought to God. They behave as if God neither knows or cares about their behaviour (v. 11). As such, the psalmist wondered why he even bothered to try and keep his heart pure (v. 13).

However, his world view dramatically changes in verse 17. In God's presence, he sees "their final destiny". The wicked may escape God's judgement now, but not forever. At death they'll "be completely swept away by terrors" (v. 19). They are on slippery ground and will tumble to destruction (vv. 18–20).

Asaph now admits he spoke in ignorance (v. 22). He comes to the same realisation as Job. Job also questioned God's justice (see Job 9:14–17; 27:2). He, too, had a revelation from God (chapters 38–41). Then he, like Asaph, admitted "I spoke of things I did not understand" (42:3).

Asaph ends off by reaffirming his relationship with God, "whom have I in heaven but you?" (v. 25). This is one of the Old Testament's clearest confessions of belief in life after death. Asaph knew God would take him to glory.

Psalm 73 doesn't answer all our questions about justice. Many people suffer in ways that seem unfair, and we long for more justice in this life. But we can take comfort in knowing that God is not removed from our sufferings. He came to us in Jesus and experienced our world of pain and injustice. After His death, He rose and now reigns in glory, "the firstfruits of those who have fallen asleep" (1 Corinthians 15:20). **When Jesus comes to judge the wicked, we can be confident that He'll receive "the pure in heart" into glory.**

Have there been times in your life when you doubted God and His kindness because of suffering and injustice? What renewed or sustained your faith?

How would you encourage someone, Christian and non-Christian, who comes to you with the same kinds of doubts and questions raised in Psalm 73?

Day 24

Read Psalm 74

We are all prone to forgetting things once in a while. When we miss an appointment, we might say, "It slipped my mind." Our human memories are fallible, prone to falter, especially as our brains age. In comparison, the Bible describes God's memory as being so much more substantial than mere mental activity. It involves an act of His will. When God remembers, He acts.

Psalm 74 expresses the psalmist's despair at the terrible suffering that has come upon Israel and God's apparent unwillingness to do anything about it. The references to the ruins of Mount Zion and the destruction of God's sanctuary (vv. 2–3) suggest that he's referring to the fall of Jerusalem at the hands of the Babylonians in 586 B.C.

The psalm begins with a request for God to remember (v. 2), in particular, to remember who is suffering. This isn't just any nation. This is Israel, the sheep of God's pasture (v. 1). God has redeemed them and chosen to dwell in their midst. Asaph doesn't think that God has mentally forgotten who His chosen people are; he is saying in essence, "Since You're our shepherd, do something!"

In verses 4–8, he describes in graphic detail the wanton destruction by

their enemies who "smashed", "burnt", and "defiled" the Holy City. The psalmist did not question God on whether or not Israel deserved this suffering. If he's referring to the destruction of Jerusalem, then we know it was a just judgment on Israel for centuries of sin and idolatry, which God has forewarned numerously through prophets like Jeremiah. The psalmist's question "how long?" (v. 10) reflects his frustration that God is silent (v. 9) about when their suffering will end.

At this point, it seems that the psalmist has lost his faith in God. But he hasn't. In verses 12–17, he reminds himself and fellow Israelites of God's mighty power, as seen in His creation of the world. **If God made everything—the sea and land, summer and winter— then He has the power to rescue His people.**

The psalm ends with seven pleas for God to act: "remember . . . do not hand over . . . do not forget . . . have regard for . . . do not let . . . rise up . . . do not ignore" (vv. 18–23). The first plea, again, is "remember" (v. 18, see also v. 22), in particular, for God to remember the covenant He made with Abraham (v. 20; see Genesis 12:1–3). The psalmist is essentially pleading with God, "You promised to bless us and make us great, please act now."

Sometimes, we, too, feel that powerful forces like the world, the flesh, and the devil are having the victory over us. Perhaps we despair. But God has promised to complete the good work He began in our lives (Philippians 1:6). If we ever think that we're fighting a losing battle alone, we can cry out to God: Remember me! Rise up and act.

Have there been times in your life when you felt like God has rejected you? What guidance does this psalm give for times like that?

What other promises has God given us in the New Testament that He will not fail us?

Day 25

Read Psalm 75

I think a lot about the kind of life I want to live. Every day I make choices so that I can have a good life. And as I get older, I think more about death. So, I eat healthier and exercise more to (hopefully) delay death. I believe most people are like me. But most days, I forget to give much thought to what comes next. Hebrews 9:27 says, "People are destined to die once, and after that to face judgment". Psalm 75 forces us to face the issue of impending judgment.

Psalm 74 posed the question, "How long will the enemy mock you, God?" (Psalm 74:10). Psalm 75 gives an answer, "I choose the appointed time; it is I who judge with equity" (75:2). One day, the mockery of the wicked will be silenced.

The psalm opens in praise of God, who is near to His people (v. 1). However, the chief cause for praise is that God has chosen the appointed time to judge the wicked with equity (v. 2). The apostle Paul echoed these thoughts when he announced to the people in Athens that, "(God) has set a day when he will judge the world with justice" (Acts 17:31).

Evil and injustice is not how things are meant to be. A world full of wickedness without justice and punishment is like a machine that isn't working properly. One day God will fix this. **His judgment will make things right again and put things back on a firm foundation (Psalm 75:3).**

The psalmist describes the wicked as arrogant, almost defying God to judge them (v. 5). He describes God's wrath as a cup full of His foaming anger about to be poured out on the ungodly (v. 8). This is a common biblical metaphor for God's judgment (see Psalm 60:3; Jeremiah 25:15–38; Nahum 1:10). In the garden of Eden, Jesus prayed that God would take away this cup from Him (Matthew 26:42). This was the cup of God's wrath for our sins that Jesus knew He would bear on the cross. Jesus drank this cup so that we who've trusted Him will never face God's wrath. But for those who have not trusted Christ, on God's appointed day, they "will drink the wine of God's fury, which has been poured full strength into the cup of his wrath" (Revelation 14:10).

A woman at my church once confessed to me that she was scared of judgment. I assured her that, if she has trusted Christ, then she has nothing to fear. For the believer, judgment day is a day that will mark our passing from this fallen world into the bliss and joy of eternal life in God's presence.

_____

_____

_____

_____

_____

_____

ThinkThrough

Psalm 75 is a song in praise of God's wrath. How might it strengthen the church if she sings more songs about judgment day? (see Revelation 11:16–18; 12:10–12; 18:1–24).

How important is it to warn people about the coming judgment in our evangelism?

_____

_____

_____

_____

_____

_____

_____

_____

_____

_____

_____

Day 26

Read Psalm 76

Have you ever heard people talk about the "victorious Christian life"? They usually mean that Christians can have victory over sin and temptation, see fruits in our ministries, experience blessing in our family life, and enjoy continual joy and peace. But when we read the Psalms, the picture is often different. The one who is victorious is God and the ones who share in His victory are weak, poor, and oppressed.

Like Psalm 68, this psalm praises God for being the Warrior who fights for His people. It appears that Jerusalem has been under attack. But the Lord has come to her defence and wonderfully defeated her enemy, because Zion was where He had chosen to dwell with His people (76:1–2).

The psalmist describes the splendour of his God. He's like a mountain—strong and immovable (v. 4). No-one can stand before such a God in battle. Interestingly, no mention is made of Israel contributing to their victory. It seems that they only had to stand back and watch God make "both horse and chariot lie still" (v. 6).

Asaph describes the victorious people as "the afflicted of the land" (v. 9). This term describes a group of people who are weak, oppressed, helpless, persecuted, and desperate. Yet, these are the victorious people of God.

There are two important lessons here for us. The Bible makes more of the victorious God than His victorious people. We have victory over sin because "our old self was crucified with him . . . that we should no longer be slaves to sin" (Romans 6:6). We have victory over Satan because Christ has disarmed the powers and authorities (Colossians 2:15). Christ conquered death so God "gives us the victory through our Lord Jesus Christ" (1 Corinthians 15:57). Every victory we enjoy has been won for us by our Warrior King.

Second, the psalmist describes the "victorious" Christian in the same way as apostle Paul. Speaking of his own ministry, Paul reminds us that, "we are hard pressed on every side, but not crushed; perplexed but not in despair; persecuted but not abandoned; struck down but not destroyed" (2 Corinthians 4:8–9). **The first quality of victorious Christians is a recognition of our own weakness.** Yet, even though the enemies arrayed against us are powerful and formidable, we know Christ has defeated them. By faith, we share in His victory.

At the end of the psalm, Asaph calls on all people to bring "gifts to the One to be feared" (Psalm 76:11). Today, we bring gifts of money or possessions so we can "do good and to share with others, for with such sacrifices God is pleased" (Hebrews 13:16).

ThinkThrough

The psalmist describes God as "radiant with light" (Psalm 76:4). What is the light of God's radiance? (see 1 John 1:5). What is the relationship between God being light and His plundering of the valiant (Psalm 76:5)?

In the New Testament, power and victory are experienced in the context of weakness (e.g. 2 Corinthians 13:4). How has that been your experience?

Day 27

Read Psalm 77

Sometimes we may be so overwhelmed by life's problems that we find it hard to see or feel evidence of God's love. In such dark moments, where do we turn?

John 3:16 tells us, "For God so loved the world that he gave his one and only Son". Notice that John says that God "loved" us, not He loves us. John's use of the past tense here doesn't mean that God doesn't love us today—He does! Rather, it places emphasis that the one undeniable and unchanging proof of God's love for us is in the gift that He has *already* given us: His Son to save us from our sins. Hence, in moments of despair, we can look back at that wonderful salvation and know that God is on our side.

Psalm 77 conveys a similar lesson. Here, the psalmist is in deep distress. He does the right thing in turning to God, but this only increases his torment because God does not comfort him (v. 2). He has endured many sleepless nights and reached a point where he can't find the words to say or the prayers to pray (v. 4). He casts his mind back to a different kind of nights when joyful songs were on his lips (vv. 5–6). But this memory only makes his present suffering even worse.

The psalmist asks God a series of questions (vv. 7–9), reminding Him that He had promised to show His people favour, mercy and compassion (vv. 7–9; see also Exodus 34:6–7). The psalmist hopes that these questions will provoke God to help him.

Verse 10 is the turning point in the psalm. Until this point, all his thoughts were about his problems. Now he decides to think differently, "I will consider all your works" (v. 12). He needs God to work a miracle in his life, so he remembers the most dramatic miracle of all. He recalls how God saved His people from Egypt, climactically through the parting of the Red Sea (vv. 14–20). **If God powerfully delivered His people then, He can deliver them today, too.**

As we read this psalm, we might feel uncomfortable at how this sufferer speaks to God. He isn't just bold, but accusatory, even disrespectful. Yet, the Lord does not rebuke him. Actually, God has ensured that this psalm is kept in the Bible for us. While there is a line not to be crossed in speaking to God (for example, Job will never curse God who he knows has permitted his trials), the presence of this psalm—

and others like it—give us divine permission to be honest in speaking to God.

Where do you go to if you feel disappointed with God? We go to the place where "with your mighty arm you redeemed your people" (v. 15). For you and me, that's the cross.

ThinkThrough

Have there been times when you've felt disappointed with God? What causes such disappointments? What Bible passages have you found helpful at such times?

What does the cross of Christ teach us about the love of God?

Day 28

Read Psalm 78

The 19th century Spanish philosopher, George Santayana, famously wrote, "Those who forget the past are condemned to repeat it". In other words, we should learn from our mistakes. We can't change what we've done, but wise people can ensure that they'll do things differently in the future.

Psalm 78 has two purposes. First, it is a "parable" (v. 2), a story that is intended to teach us how to live wisely. Like the writers of Proverbs, the psalmist is a man who is passing on "things we have heard and known" (v. 3)—namely, lessons from Israel's history—to future generations.

The poet begins by reminding his readers that God had given the law to enable them to trust and stay faithful to Him (vv. 5–8). However, Israel had a history of repeatedly sinning against God and putting Him to the test. They kept forgetting what God had done for them, "the wonders he had shown them" (v. 11): God's saving power in sending plagues on Egypt, dividing the Red Sea, providing bread and food in the wilderness, and giving them the promised land (vv. 12–16; 23–29; 42–55). Their failure to remember God's goodness led to a failure to live in the right way again and again. Yet, even though He punished them for their sin (vv. 59–64), God didn't give up on them because He knew they were weak (v. 39).

The second purpose in Psalm 78 is to show that God will not allow this cycle of sin, judgment, and forgiveness to continue. He has acted decisively to change the future. He has chosen to live amongst His people in His sanctuary (vv. 68–69) and, more importantly, chosen David to shepherd His people "with integrity of heart" (v. 72).

This psalm, like so many others, drives us to Jesus. Even God's chosen shepherd, David, failed and compromised his integrity. But our one true king, Jesus, is the good Shepherd who leads and protects us perfectly.

Hebrews 2:3 warns Christians, "how shall we escape if we ignore so great a salvation". We must pass on to the next generation the parable of the wonders of our salvation, which is all that Jesus has done for us to bring us to God and give us eternal life. **Preachers and teachers in the church need to remind our people about the parable of their salvation regularly, so they will remember what Jesus has done for them and live in the right way.**

ThinkThrough

What are some of the things that cause us to forget what God has done for us and not live in the light of that?

How can you pass on to the next generation the wonderful story of your salvation?

Read Psalm 79

As Christians we can expect persecution. However, Peter warns us that we should ensure that, if we do suffer, it is for doing good (1 Peter 3:13–17) and not for making poor, ungodly choices. If a Christian is insulted and called a hypocrite for behaving badly in the workplace, that's not persecution. It is only when we are persecuted "because of righteousness" that we are blessed (Matthew 5:10).

The worst suffering that Israel endured in biblical times is arguably the destruction of her city in 586 B.C. This suffering was entirely deserved. This is the likely background to Psalm 79. Similar to Psalm 74, this psalm is a lament by the survivors of this catastrophe. The psalmist begins by reminding God that it was *your* inheritance, *your* temple, *your* servants, and *your* people who were destroyed (Psalm 79:1–2). Since these people and places belong to God and are precious to Him, the poet cries out to God to come and help them.

Asaph doesn't deny that Israel's suffering is God's just punishment for their sin. But his question is, "will you be angry for ever" (v. 5)? The children of the generation that had turned away from God are still bearing the consequences of their parents' sins (v. 8). This is Asaph's lament.

The psalmist prays for two things. First, he seeks God's forgiveness (v. 9). He wants the punishment by God to end so they can begin to rebuild their lives. Secondly, he asks God to "pour out your wrath on the nations" (v. 6; see also vv. 11–12). Israel may have deserved the suffering, which came upon them for persisting in disobedience towards God, but those who murdered and destroyed brutally also deserve God's judgment.

Why should God act for Israel now? Again, there are two reasons. First, "for your name's sake" (v. 9). The poet's concern is the nations will not give God the glory He deserves. Instead they may think that God isn't strong enough to rescue them. Secondly, God's deliverance will result in the praise of His people "from generation to generation" (v. 13).

Historically, the prayer of this psalm was answered when the nation that had brought such suffering on Israel, Babylon, was destroyed in 539 B.C. The following year Israel was allowed to return and rebuild Jerusalem.

Henry Martyn (1781–1812) was a missionary to India. He was deeply hurt that the nations did not worship the Saviour of the world and wrote, "I could not endure existence if Jesus was not glorified". The writer of our psalm shares the same grief. His desire is for God to rescue them from their distress so the nations will glorify God for His power and love. **Whether we are suffering or not, God's glory should be the ultimate goal of our prayers and desire of our hearts.**

ThinkThrough

Why does the psalmist pray for deliverance and forgiveness "for your name's sake"? How does our salvation glorify the name of God?

In the light of this psalm how might you pray for the persecuted church?

Day 30

Read Psalm 80

Luke 2:25–38 introduces us to two special people, Simeon and Anna. They spend their days in the temple worshipping and praying. Simeon, in particular, is looking for "the consolation of Israel" (Luke 2:25), that is, for God to save His people. When Simeon holds the newborn Christ in his arms, he announces with joy, "my eyes have seen your salvation" (v. 30). Hundreds of years before a poet had prayed to God, "come and save us" (Psalm 80:2) and now God has fully answered that prayer.

The psalm begins with Asaph asking God to restore the people. He wants God to smile upon His people and save them (v. 3).

Again, we hear the desperate cry, "How long?" (v. 4; see 79:5). We often pray, "Give us today our daily bread" to ask God to meet our daily needs. But for the Israelites, the only bread God has given is the bread of tears (v. 5). And to rub salt into the wounds, their enemies make fun of them (v. 6).

In vv. 8–16, the psalmist takes God on a brief historical tour. Through the popular metaphor of the vine, which stands for Israel, he reminds God of the ups and the downs of their relationship with Him. God saved Israel from Egypt (v. 8) and then planted her in the promised land where she prospered (vv. 9–11).

Then the psalmist speaks of how God turned against Israel. He asks, why has this happened to us (v. 12)?

Has Asaph forgotten the centuries of idolatry and disobedience committed by Israel? Of course not. The previous two psalms have already reminded Israel of her persistent sin (see Psalm 78:32; 79:8–9). The thrust of this psalm is then a plaintive cry for God to rescue them, a note on which he both begins and ends, "Restore us, O God; make your face shine upon us, that we may be saved" (vv. 3, 19).

For centuries, the Jewish people sang this song—a prayer for salvation. Their enemies came and went, but they rarely experienced freedom and peace. Yet they never stopped praying, "Save us", because they never stopped hoping and believing.

Many churches read this psalm during Christmastime. This season reminds us of the day God finally answered the prayer of Psalm 80 through the gift of a Saviour. **Jesus Christ demonstrates that God has indeed shone His face upon us and come to save us.**

This psalm encourages us to keep praying, especially for the salvation of our loved ones. Maybe tears have been your bread for years, but keep praying because one day, like Simeon, you may discover that your prayer has been heard.

ThinkThrough

What kept many in Israel praying for salvation for centuries? How can this encourage us to be persistent in prayer, especially for our final restoration (see Revelation 6:9–11)?

Who have you been praying for a long time? Take a few moments now and use the words of Psalm 80 to guide you in praying for them.

Read Psalm 81

Christians know God personally. When we talk about our relationship with God, we usually tell our side of the story. We share our thoughts and feelings about Him. Like us, most of the psalmists express their thoughts, laments, and delights. Most of the psalms are songs of their life and experience of God. But in Psalm 81, it is God who speaks.

Most of Asaph's psalms have been laments. Psalm 81, however, opens on a note of exuberant praise, "Sing for joy to God . . . shout aloud" (v. 1). It is sung at one of Israel's festivals, where the chief cause for celebration is God's wonderful deliverance of His people from Egypt (v. 5).

The psalm takes a surprising turn when the psalmist hears "an unknown voice" (v. 5). As the following verses make clear: it is God's voice. God reminds Israel of His love for them demonstrated in setting them free and responding to their cries of distress (vv. 6–7).

However, God sadly laments, "my people would not listen to me" (v. 11). One scholar translates the second half of that verse as "they did not want me". One can almost hear the pain in God's voice. His people have turned their backs on God, who loved them and gave them everything. Yet they broke the first commandment,

"you shall have no other gods before me" (Deuteronomy 5:7). **Idolatry has always been humanity's primary act of rebellion against God (see Romans 1:18–23).**

Again and again, we can hear the emotion behind God's pleading for His people to worship Him alone. "If you would only listen to me" (Psalm 81:8; see also v. 13), He says, so that He could pour His blessings on them. He would deliver them from all their enemies (vv. 10, 14), and satisfy their hunger with the finest foods (v. 16). In the wilderness, God gave them water from a rock when they grumbled (Exodus 17:1–7). But if they had repented and returned to Him then, symbolically, the rock would have brought forth sweet honey. The psalm ends with God inviting them to join Him at His table for such a feast (Psalm 81:16).

Relationships are risky. There is always a risk of rejection and that is painful. While we cannot presume to comprehend all of God's emotions, this psalm gives us a glimpse of God's sorrow that Israel would not listen to His pleas to return to Him (Psalm 81:8). Jesus expressed the same pain in His cry over Jerusalem (Matthew 23:37–39). Similarly, Paul tells us that our sins grieve the Spirit of God (Ephesians 4:30). Never forget that God is love; He is full of divine emotion.

ThinkThrough

Read Psalm 81:12. How did God punish Israel for rejecting Him? Does God sometimes treat people in the same way today? (see Romans 1:24–32).

How do you feel when someone spurns your love? What insights might that give you into the heart of God?

Day 32

Read Psalm 82

It is generally recognised that the modern missionary movement began in 1793 when the Baptist missionary, William Carey, went to India. He went there to "convert the heathen". Through translating the Bible into the native languages, he brought the good news of Jesus to the people of India. While he was there, Carey observed ordinary people enduring great sufferings and injustice. He couldn't sit back and do nothing. He worked tirelessly to "defend the weak . . . uphold the cause of the poor . . . rescue the weak and the needy" (Psalm 82:3–4). For example, he campaigned for the humane treatment of lepers who were often buried alive. He also helped abolish the *sati*, the practice of burning widows alive on the funeral pyres of their dead husbands, and made it illegal to leave sick or unwanted babies exposed to die. William Carey exemplified the character of the "gods" as described in this psalm.

Psalm 82 is a difficult psalm to understand, although its main message is clear. The psalm begins by describing God as dwelling in "the great assembly . . . among the gods" (v. 1). What is this assembly and who are these gods? There are two popular answers to these questions.

The first view is that they are angels and the great assembly is in heaven.

Job chapter 1 describes Satan as entering the heavenly court with the angels or "the sons of the Most High" (v. 6; see Job 1:6). If this is correct, then maintaining justice and caring for the vulnerable is part of the angels' ministry (vv. 2–4). Some angels, however, failed to do so and God's punishment is that "they will fall like every other ruler" (v. 7). This explains the presence of fallen angels or demons.

The second view is that the "gods" are human judges. Their first work in the great assembly of Israel was to uphold justice and defend the cause of the weak.

It is very difficult to discern which view, among others, is correct. But whether God is rebuking heavenly hosts or earthly leaders, His complaint is clear: they have not cared for those in need.

This stands in contrast to one of Jesus' best-known parables. In the story of the Good Samaritan (Luke 10:25–37), a man is beaten and left to die. He needs rescue. Two men, teachers and leaders in Israel, walk by. But a Samaritan fulfils the will of God and rescues the weak. Jesus' command us to "go and do likewise" (v. 37).

The Bible tells us to do good to all people, especially to those of the household of faith (Galatians 6:10). As the parable in Luke 10 instructs, and as Psalm 82 makes clear, this is not an optional extra for anyone who calls himself or herself a child of God.

ThinkThrough

Who are the weak, fatherless, poor, oppressed, and needy in your world? How is God calling you to rescue them?

Read John 10:33–36 where Jesus cites Psalm 82:6. How does Jesus use this verse to support His claim to be God?

Day 33

Read Psalm 83

Matthew 10 records one time when Jesus sent out His disciples on a mission to the neighbouring towns. He knew they would face violent opposition. He said, "I am sending you out like sheep among wolves" (Matthew 10:16). It's a surprising and unsettling picture. The shepherd's job is to protect his sheep from wolves. But here the Good Shepherd deliberately sends His servants into danger. Sheep among wolves are defenceless against wolves' sharp teeth and claws. This picture of power and savagery against weakness and frailty is, for many Christians, a depiction of the world they live in today. It was also the world of Psalm 83.

The lament of Psalm 83 is familiar to readers of the psalms. Israel's enemies are threatening to destroy her (v. 4). The psalmist begs God to come and save them but God remains silent (v. 1). He reminds God of how He saved them in the past. This time he recalls some of God's powerful victories in the days of the judges. God defeated the Canaanites when Deborah was the judge (vv. 9–10), and the Midianites when Gideon was leader of the army (vv. 11–12). Finally, he prays for the humiliating overthrow of these nations (vv. 13–18).

The psalm provides us with two truths to cling to as we live in this perilous world. First, the psalmist acknowledges that Israel's enemies are God's enemies (vv. 2, 5). When the nations plot against Israel, they are plotting against God. On another occasion when Jesus sent His disciples out on a mission trip, He told them, "whoever listens to you listens to me; whoever rejects you rejects me; but whoever rejects me rejects him who sent me" (Luke 10:16). What was true of Israel is true of the church today. To attack the people of God is to attack God himself.

Second, there will be a day when God's enemies will be terrified by His judgment (Psalm 83:15). The ultimate purpose is not for vengeance, but so that they will know that "you alone are the Most High over all the earth" (v. 18). **As Christians, it should be our desire to see God's enemies repent of their evil ways and joyfully submit to the Lord.** We proclaim the wrath to come so that unbelievers may "serve the living and true God" (1 Thessalonians 1:9).

There's a story of an American Coast Guard who was sent out into a hurricane to rescue a ship that was breaking up just off the coast. The captain told his men to prepare to go out to sea. One sailor replied, "But Captain, we may never come back."

The Captain said, "Son, you don't have to come back. You have to go out." God calls us to serve Him in a hostile and dangerous world, whatever the cost.

ThinkThrough

What has been your experience of the attacks by "wolves" (see Psalm 83:2)? What can we learn from Psalm 83 about how to respond at such times?

Why would God's enemies "be ashamed and dismayed" (Psalm 83:17)? What is shameful about opposing God?

Day 34

Read Psalm 84

Thus far, we have read eleven psalms by Asaph, most of which are laments. They are cries for help from sinful people who feel God is far away. However, the tone changes dramatically as we read Psalm 84, written by the sons of Korah. Almost every verse throb with joy, excitement, and rapture.

At least once a year, Jews would go to the temple in Jerusalem to worship and celebrate a feast. Most commentators believe this psalm was written for these pilgrims to sing on the journey.

The psalm begins in joyful praise of the splendour of the temple. The temple was both renowned for its breathtaking beauty and for being the dwelling place of God. Hence, the singers' desire to be in the temple reflects a desire to be near God. The writer even envies the birds who build their nests near the altar (Psalm 84:3). Like them, he'd love to live in the temple every day (not that people actually lived in the temple).

In verses 5–7, he remembers his journey to the temple as they pass through the Valley of Baka (or "weeping"). In poetic language, the psalmist imagines the dry land turning fertile as the pilgrims approach the temple. It's as if the people and creation join together in joyful celebration of their God.

The singers then pray for their king, the "anointed one" (v. 9). Israel's great hope was to dwell with God under His chosen king, who would rule in justice and righteousness.

The psalmist concludes with the joyful confession that there's nowhere else he'd rather be than in God's temple (v. 10). He ends with a blessing on all who obey (v. 11) and trust God (v. 12), implying that's what we should all do.

For four months, my daughter studied in Jerusalem. She loved her time in that special city. I have many friends who have found visits to Israel a spiritually enriching experience. Of course, there is no temple in Jerusalem now. Jesus foretold its destruction (Mark 13:1–2). He announced the end of the physical temple because He, the true temple, had come (John 2:19–22). **Today, we don't go to a building to meet God. We go to Jesus in whom the whole fullness of God dwells (Colossians 1:19).** For Christians, everything we read here about the temple is true of Jesus. I'd rather spend a day serving Him than a lifetime serving sin and Satan.

It's also true that together, Christians are the temple of God (1 Corinthians 3:16). Our desire to be in the presence of God should be expressed in our desire to regularly gather with the people of God. This psalm is a reminder of the joy and privilege of being part of God's church.

Read through this psalm again. How does it express the splendour and beauty of the Lord Jesus and our love for him?

What can we do to reflect the joy of Psalm 84 in our church life?

Day 35

When my wife and I moved into our inner-city apartment, it was a mess. The previous tenants had wrecked it. It was dirty and things were broken. The apartment needed restoration. We repainted and recarpeted it. We renovated the kitchen, laundry, and bathroom. Sometimes, similar to our apartment, we are in need of restoration. Our lives are a mess, sometimes caused by our own doing. The poet in Psalm 85 finds himself in a similar predicament.

Yet, in Psalm 85, although the poet asks God to restore his fortunes, his pleas are not just for personal restoration. Psalm 85 is a prayer for the renewal of the nation. The nation is suffering. There is no peace or *shalom*. For Israel, "peace" meant to live prosperously in the land God had given them, free from the fear of enemies. But this was not her present experience and now she knows why. Her sins have angered God (v. 5). So, the psalmist looks back to when God forgave their sins in the past and restored them (vv. 1–3) and asks God to "revive us again" (v. 6).

The psalmist knows that the people need to do two things in order for the Lord to again "grant us your salvation" (v. 7). Firstly, they must "fear him" (v. 9). **Fearing God means recognising His rightful rule over our lives and the terrible consequence of His "fierce anger" (v. 3) if we disobey Him.** Disobedience is foolish and so, secondly, the nation must "not turn to folly" (v. 8). Pursuing folly means forgetting to fear God.

After numerous pleas for forgiveness and restoration, the psalm ends on a wonderful note of hope. Verse 10 is one of the most beautiful verses in Psalms. "Love and faithfulness meet together" is a picture of mutual delight as God's love and His people's obedience embrace each other. This love is God's love for us shown in the covenant promises He made to be our God and bless us. Faithfulness, which "springs forth from the earth" (v. 11), is our response to this love. We are His faithful servants (v. 8). The second half of verse 10 repeats this truth with an even more intimate picture, "righteousness and peace kiss each other". God's righteousness, which is His commitment to keep His promises to bless His people, "looks down from heaven" (v. 11) and brings the peace or *shalom* the people are longing for.

Salvation is the meeting of love and faithfulness. God the Father reached out to us in love, and God the Son, His perfectly faithful servant, was obedient to the point of death on the cross. The result is the wonderful peace we now enjoy. Do you need renewal and restoration? Go to the cross, where love and faithfulness met.

_____

_____

_____

_____

_____

_____

_____

Have there been times in your life when you felt you needed restoration? Why did you feel that way? How did the Lord restore you?

What encourage-ment could you bring from this psalm to someone who is longing for personal spiritual renewal?

_____

_____

_____

_____

_____

_____

_____

_____

_____

_____

Day 36

Read Psalm 86

Recently, a friend of mine told me that he'd joined a church, "because [he] was broken". His life was full of sorrow and hurt. So, he turned to God his Saviour. His decision echoes King David's when he, too, turned to the Lord in his "poor and needy" state (Psalm 86:1). As David had arrogant and ruthless people trying to kill him (v. 14), he asks God to save him (v. 16) and give him joy again (v. 4).

Two things stand out in this psalm. First, David affirms the uniqueness of God. Every nation has its idols. In David's day, there were gods like Baal. In Paul's day, it was the gods of Greece and Rome. In today's world, we put our trust in things like money. In times of trouble, people turn to these gods for help. David confesses that God has no equal "among the gods" (v. 8). **Whether we worship gods made of stone or dollar bills, they are all just worthless idols. God alone is true for "no deeds can compare with yours" (v. 8).**

As David praises this mighty God, he sees a day when, not just the nation of Israel, but all the nations will worship Him alone (v. 9). In Revelation 15, John is given a vision of the victorious saints praising God for His holiness. They sing these words from Psalm 86:9.

The hope that David expressed in the psalm is becoming a reality "for your righteous acts have been revealed" (Revelation 15:4). One day everyone will acknowledge their gods are false. They will worship the one true God whose saving power sets His people free from bondage to sin, Satan, and the fear of death.

In the psalms, the poet typically calls on God to save him and then at the end of the psalm expresses his hope for deliverance. However, Psalm 86 is different. The psalm begins, "Hear me, LORD" (v. 1) and ends, "give me a sign" (v. 17). In other words, David still hasn't seen his prayer answered. His praise of God comes in the midst of his suffering. He doesn't wait for rescue to happen before praising God with all his heart (v. 12). David's deepest desire is for the Lord to teach him His way (v. 11). What is more important to David is the health of his soul rather than the saving of his life. Then, with a heart fully focussed on the Lord, David will learn more of godly fear and make the glory of God his chief goal in life (v. 12).

It's easy to praise God after a wonderful answer to prayer. The mark of a man or woman with "an undivided heart" (v. 11) is when, in the midst of great suffering, they can boldly affirm, "for great is your love towards me" (v. 13).

ThinkThrough

What are the false gods of your society? What does worship of these gods look like?

How is it possible, in the midst of great trouble, to maintain our spiritual priorities and continue to affirm the goodness and love of the Lord?

Day 37

Read Psalm 87

Whenever we read the Old Testament, we need to remember that we are reading God's promises to His people that find their ultimate fulfilment in Christ. The Old Testament points forward to Jesus Christ and finds its true meaning in Him. It builds up our sure expectation that the Messiah will soon arrive. This is especially true in Psalm 87.

Psalm 87 praises Zion, the mountain on which Jerusalem was built. Of course, Jerusalem existed long before it became "the holy mountain" (v. 1). After David conquered the city (2 Samuel 5:6–12), he expressed his desire to build the temple there (7:1–2). The temple was symbolically God's dwelling place, the place where God chose to make His presence felt. God's presence in Zion made it the glorious "city of God" (Psalm 87:3).

Verses 4–6 are prophetic. The psalmist looks forward to the day when people from the pagan nations, like Egypt ("Rahab" is a poetic name for Egypt) and Babylon, become citizens of Zion. One day, God's enemies will become His friends and worship Him in His presence. They'll be listed in the register of those who belong to God (v. 4; see Revelation 20:12–15), and find the fountain of life and salvation in the city of God (Psalm 87:7).

The temple in Jerusalem is no more. **We can now worship God in spirit and in truth at any place (John 4:21–24), because of Christ's completed work on the cross.** And since all God's people are in Christ, Paul can describe the church as "God's temple" (1 Corinthians 3:16).

Revelation gives us a glorious picture of the new Jerusalem (Revelation 21:9–27). I believe it's not a literal city. It is the people of God, the bride of Christ: "Come, I will show you the bride, the wife of the Lamb . . . and showed me the Holy City" (vv. 9–10; see also 19:7–8). The glory of the heavenly Zion is the glory of the transformed people of God. All the images of the city are symbolical. *We* are the gates made of pearl (v. 21), a people who are pure and resplendent. *We* are the streets of gold, a people precious in His sight.

How do Christians sing Psalm 87? First, we glory in the Lord Jesus, in whom the whole fullness of God dwells in bodily form (Colossians 2:9). Jesus is the fountain of life for all who know Him. Second, as Christians we can rejoice that we are the city of God. How amazing is the grace of God that the Lord of heaven and earth has made His home in us! That's worth singing about.

ThinkThrough

In light of the fulfilment of this psalm in the person of Jesus, what does it mean, "This one was born in Zion" (Psalm 87:6)?

Read Revelation 21:9–27. Make a list of the glorious features of the Holy City, which is the heavenly people of God.

Day 38

Read Psalm 88

In my country, Australia, one in seven people will experience depression at some time in their life, and one-quarter will experience an anxiety condition. According to the World Health Organization, across the world about 300 million people of all ages are currently suffering from depression.

Psalm 88 powerfully expresses the painful suffering of those who are depressed. We've seen that as many as a half of all the psalms are laments or contain some lament. But no psalm is as bleak and despairing as Psalm 88. Its context in the book of Psalms deliberately highlights its sense of despair. Psalm 87 ends with the words, "As they make music they will sing, 'All my fountains are in you'" (v. 7), and Psalm 89 begins, "I will sing of the LORD's great love for ever" (v. 1). Psalm 88 almost seems to mock the joyful praises in the songs that come before and after it.

Like so many of the laments, Heman the songwriter keeps the specific details of his "troubles" (Psalm 88:3) from us. This suggests that he is more concerned about the pain that they cause him. Heman points his finger squarely at God, "you have put me in the lowest pit" (v. 6); "you have overwhelmed me with all your waves" (v. 7); "you have taken from me my closest friends" (v. 8). Like

Job, Heman knows and confesses that "the LORD gave and the LORD has taken away" (Job 1:21). But unlike Job he cannot yet say, "may the name of the LORD be praised" and blames God for being the ultimate cause of his troubles.

How does a Christian who has experienced God's amazing love and grace in the Lord Jesus respond to Psalm 88? First, we must acknowledge that there may be times in our life when we feel that "darkness is [our] closest friend" (v. 18). Some believers sadly suffer with clinical depression. Just last week, I read of a godly young pastor who had suffered from depression and tragically took his life. Christians will go through times of physical or mental suffering, bereavement, failure, disappointment, or persecution. We may feel that God has hidden His face from us.

Psalm 88 gives us permission to cry out loudly to the Lord. Repeatedly, Heman calls out to God (vv. 2, 9, 13). **For all his pain, Heman never stops praying. He may feel God has turned His face against him but he continues to turn his face towards God.**

Heman only had the vaguest understanding of life beyond the

grave (vv. 10–12). We, though, know that a day is coming when God will wipe away every tear from our eyes. Because Jesus died and rose again, we have a certain hope that our darkness will end "for the Lord God will give them light" (Revelation 22:5).

Psalm 88 is a brutally honest psalm. Do Christians sometimes wear a mask to hide their doubts, questions, and anger at God? Why? How does Psalm 88 address this situation?

In the light of this psalm, how could you comfort someone who is angry with God and feels that "darkness is my closest friend" (Psalm 88:18)?

Day 39

Read Psalm 89

It's not surprising that Christians often ask, why has God done this in my life? If He is faithful and kind, why does He appear so cruel? Why are prayers unanswered when God has promised He will answer? We must not give black-or-white answers like, "you didn't have enough faith". The reality is that, sometimes, the ways of God seem unfair and, in this life, we may never know why. Like many other psalms, Psalm 89 addresses this issue.

Psalm 89 surprises us. It almost seems like two diametrically opposed psalms. It begins as a psalm of praise by singing of God's great love and faithfulness (vv. 1–2). This love was shown particularly when a covenant was established with David, promising him a lasting dynasty (vv. 3–4).

The psalmist then exalts God as supreme among all the heavenly beings (vv. 5–8), the creator and powerful ruler of heaven and earth (vv. 9–13).

All this forms a backdrop to the central part of this psalm where the writer remembers how God chose David to be both the people's king and His own firstborn son (v. 27; see 1 Samuel 16). While the Lord will discipline any of David's descendants who "fail to keep [His] commands" (v. 31–32), nevertheless He has promised to never "violate my covenant" (v. 34). David's line will continue for ever (vv. 35–37).

Then in v. 38 there is a dramatic change in tone, "But you have rejected . . . your anointed one". The accusation is fierce—that God has broken His promise. We don't know what crisis prompted the writer's outburst, but the nation is under threat from enemies. It appears the end of the rule of the kingdom of David is near. The psalm concludes with a plea for God to change His attitude and take action (vv. 50–51).

The fact is that the line of David came to an end with the fall of Jerusalem in 586 B.C. Had God broken His promise? It certainly looked like it. However, the prophets foretell a future son of David who would reign for ever (see Isaiah 11:1–5; Jeremiah 23:5–6). The good news of the New Testament is that the true "son of David" has come and God's faithful people recognised Him (see Matthew 9:27; Luke 1:32; Acts 13:22–23). The New Testament ends with the promise of the second coming of the "Offspring of David" (Revelation 22:16).

To the writer of Psalm 89, it looked like God had broken His word. Today we can see that He was always faithful to the promise of providing an eternal king. **In the same way, one day we'll be able to look back and see how the Lord was working out His good purposes in our lives even when it didn't look like it.**

ThinkThrough

Have there been times in your life when it looked like God was unkind or unfaithful? Were you able to talk to God? What did you say?

Like Psalm 88, the writer of Psalm 89 does not end on a note of hope or trust. How is our situation different because of Christ Jesus?

Read Psalm 90

The famous evangelist, Billy Graham, was asked what most surprised him in life. He answered, "Its brevity." Psalm 90 is a brutally honest psalm in which Moses reflects on God's eternity and, in the light of that, our mortality.

Psalm 90 begins Book 4 of Psalms. It is the only psalm written by the great lawgiver, Moses. The title is, "The prayer of Moses the man of God." It's a poem or prayer in three parts.

Verses 1–6 lay the necessary foundation for what is to follow. God is unceasingly faithful to His people. Moses stands in awe at the fact of God's eternal existence. But this isn't just a comforting reminder to him, it's also a sobering reminder of humanity's brief life. If God is forever, we pass in the blink of an eye. This puts our contemporary boastings about a long life into perspective. We boast that we might live for 100 years, but this is barely "a watch in the night" against God's eternity (v. 4).

In verses 7–12, Moses isn't satisfied to simply reflect on the shortness of our days. He confronts us with the equally unpleasant fact of what these days are like. They are full of sorrow and turmoil (vv. 9–10). His words take us back to Genesis 3 and God's judgment on men and women because of sin. God had

said, "Cursed is the ground because of you; through painful toil you will eat food from it all the days of your life" (Genesis 3:17). Humanity's work would be hard and frustrating. And glorious childbirth would come in terrible agony (v. 16). Why is life like this? Moses reminds us that it's because of sin and God's anger (Psalm 90:7–9).

So, stop, says Moses. Sit down and take a good hard look at life. Pull out your calculator and do your sums. Learn wisdom from the brevity and bleakness of life (v. 12).

Since sin is the root cause of our troubles, the solution is divine compassion (v. 13). Moses' prayer doesn't end with despair (vv. 13–17). He prays for his people to know God's unfailing love so they can "be glad all our days" (v. 14).

Moses never lived to see the answer to his prayer. He couldn't foresee a day when our brief lives would turn into eternal life, and our sorrow transformed into joy. While Moses longed for the day when he could "sing for joy" (v. 14), every Christmas Christians sing, "Joy to the world the Lord has come". What Moses could only pray, we see and experience in the cross of Christ. It was there that our sins, both open and secret (v. 8) were washed away. **On the cross, Jesus was consumed by God's anger (v. 7) so that the favour of the Lord might rest on us (v. 17).**

ThinkThrough

Do you agree that much of life is "but trouble and sorrow" (Psalm 90:10)? What insights do Psalm 90 give us into the character of life in a fallen world?

What are the spiritual benefits of numbering our days?

Day 41

Read Psalm 91

Psalm 91 expresses confidence in God to protect His people in all kinds of trouble. However, it raises more questions than it gives answers. It seems to stand in stark contrast to the previous three psalms. In Psalm 88, the poet is "overwhelmed with troubles" (v. 3). Psalms 89 and 90 both affirm that life is fleeting (Psalm 89:47; 90:5) and full of sorrow (90:10). Yet, Psalm 91 promises that those who love God won't even strike their foot against a stone (91:12) and will be blessed with a long life (v. 16). How does a Christian understand and sing Psalm 91?

The psalm begins by promising us that we will be kept safe because God is our shelter (v. 1). The psalmist identifies two threats to our life and safety: plague and war (vv. 3, 6–7). However, from what he later writes, we know that he's claiming God's protection from anything and everything that can harm us (vv. 11–13). The poet uses the popular Old Testament image of the Lord as a bird, under whose wings we find refuge, to describe God's protection (v. 4; see also 17:8; 36:7; 57:1; 61:4; 63:7). The psalm concludes by assuring all those who love God that He will deliver them from all their troubles and, finally, give them salvation (vv. 15–16).

The psalmist's words appear to contradict what many of us experience. I spent 11 years in missionary service. I experienced suffering as a result of following Christ—I repeatedly fell sick; I experienced frustration and failure. I also realised that suffering is often the pathway to Christian maturity. In the light of experience and the rest of Scripture, how can we understand Psalm 91?

First, the book before Psalms is Job. Job testifies that sometimes God, in His mysterious wisdom, will allow His faithful servants to suffer terribly. The writer of Psalm 91 knew this. So, he is not denying that "in this world you will have trouble" (John 16:33).

Second, for us today, the fullest understanding of the meaning of Psalm 91 is spiritual. For example, the apostle Paul was not protected from beatings, stoning, imprisonments, and shipwrecks, but he knew all these hardships "will turn out for my deliverance" (Philippians 1:19). In the Lord's prayer, we ask God to "lead us not into temptation" (Matthew 6:13; the Greek word for "temptation" can also mean testing) and He does. While Satan attacks us, God will always rescue and protect His people (Revelation 12:13–17; Luke 22:31–32). And those who love God will enjoy a long life; indeed, the certain hope of a believer is eternal life.

In the second temptation of Jesus, the devil quoted Psalm 91:11–12 (see Matthew 4:5–7). Jesus refused to put God to the test. While this psalm applies to everyone who trusts God, preeminently it applied to Jesus. He knew suffering. His life was cut short. Yet He rose from the dead. **Spiritual protection and bodily resurrection are the ultimate promise of this psalm and the hope of all believers.**

ThinkThrough

What advice would you give to a friend who takes every promise in this psalm literally, such as "no disaster will ever come near your tent" (Psalm 91:10)?

What do you understand about the role and ministry of angels (Psalm 91:11; see also Matthew 18:10; 26:53; Hebrews 13:2)?

Day 42

Read Psalm 92

I am passionate about the importance of congregational singing, so much that I've written articles and a book (*The Songs of the Saints*) about the topic. I believe Christians need to understand why we sing and learn to sing good songs well. Psalm 92 is the only psalm dedicated to the Sabbath and it gives us something to sing about when we meet as God's saved people.

The psalmist begins by acknowledging that it's good to praise God (v. 1). When we sing, we preach! We proclaim His love and faithfulness (v. 2). God demonstrated these twin virtues in two ways. First, in His great works (v. 5). This psalm doesn't specify exactly the Lord's wonderful saving deeds for His people (see Psalm 136), but those who remembered Israel's history knew them. The Lord is also praised for His profound thoughts (v. 5). In a similar context of salvation and blessing, Isaiah also blesses God, whose ways and thoughts are higher than ours (Isaiah 55:6–13).

The psalmist now gives two examples of God's great works. They are seen, firstly, in the destruction of His enemies. God's enemies are also the psalmist's enemies. For a while, they may seem to have the upper hand, but ultimately, they will perish (Psalm 92:6–9). Secondly, the righteous will be lifted up. Like the horn of an ox, he will know strength, and he will experience joy and refreshment as with fine oils poured on him (v. 10).

The theme of the flourishing of the righteous marks the final part of the psalm (vv. 12–15). With words reminiscent of Psalm 1, the psalmist celebrates the joy of flourishing in God's presence. He likens the prosperity of the righteous to the palm tree and the cedar. Old Testament scholar Tremper Longman notes that both the palm tree and the cedar were represented in the temple. The temple was built of cedar (1 Kings 5), and it contained symbols of the palm tree (6:29). As Longman says, "the righteous themselves flourish in the presence of God".

We have come a long way from the bleak and complaining laments of Psalms 88 and 89. Such psalms are necessary because they remind us of how difficult it can be to keep trusting God in the midst of suffering and frustration. But now, with Psalms 91 and 92, light has dawned on the psalmist's dark night of the soul. **Whatever our situation, "it is good to praise the Lord" (Psalm 92:1) and put into words why God is worthy of our praise.** When we sing, we are both praising God and proclaiming to Him and to one another, "the LORD is upright; he is my Rock" (v. 15).

_____

_____

_____

_____

ThinkThrough

What are the great works of God that you have experienced in your life? Turn these words into praise.

What are the profound thoughts of God that make Him worthy of praise? Turn these words into praise.

_____

_____

_____

_____

_____

_____

_____

_____

_____

_____

_____

_____

_____

Day 43

Read Psalm 93

One of the great blessings that a society can experience is a stable and strong government. Some governments come and go quickly because of internal political conflict or coups. Other governments might be corrupt, lack any vision, or have insufficient means to enact their policies. As a result, the economy falters. Crime rises. Poverty spreads. The nation becomes vulnerable to attack or outside influences. In contrast, a good and strong government promotes order in society and consequently, peace, safety, and prosperity.

Psalm 93 is the first of a number of psalms (Psalms 95–99) that praises God for being the King over all the earth. One of the most important and comforting truths in the Bible is that God is sovereign. "The Lord reigns" (Psalm 93:1) over everyone and everything and, ultimately, all people and all events serve His purposes. **Unlike kings who rule for a lifetime or presidents who rule for a fixed term of office, God reigns forever.** Since He is the King, the world is "firm and secure" (v. 1). In other words, while there are wars and natural disasters, God manages all these things to ensure the wellbeing and survival of His creation.

In the myths and stories of the ancient world, the sea was often portrayed as a symbol of chaos. Similarly, in Genesis 1:2, we are told that "darkness was over the surface of the deep . . . over the waters" before God spoke and brought order. Some of us have experienced violent sea storms, floods, or a tsunami. The waters seem uncontrollable. But the Lord is "mightier than the breakers of the sea" (Psalm 93:4). Indeed, these forces of chaos "have lifted up their voice" (v. 3) in praise of the One who made them and rules them. So, if the Lord controls the powerful, terrifying waters, we can be confident in His rule over all the forces on earth.

How does the King of all creation rule the peoples of the earth? The psalm concludes by telling us, "your statutes, Lord, stand firm" (v. 5). By His law, enacted through His appointed human kings, God rules His people, promoting order and restraining evil.

Jesus is "Lord of lords and King of kings" (Revelation 17:14). He rules His kingdom by His Word (see Matthew 28:18–20). Twice in His ministry, Jesus displayed His divine power over the terrifying chaos of the sea when He stilled a storm (8:23–27) and walked on water (John 6:16–21). Under His government, there is "righteousness, peace, and joy in the Holy Spirit" (Romans 14:17).

Have you ever experienced life under an unstable government? What was it like? Have you experienced life under a good government? What was that like?

What is life like in a church which acknowledges Jesus as King and lives under the authority of His Word?

Day 44

Read Psalm 94

I n Psalm 93, the poet rejoiced in the sovereign and holy God who rules His world. The world is "firm and secure" when the Lord reigns (v. 1). But what is life like under corrupt and cruel rulers? Psalm 94 paints a dark picture of the suffering of people when there is "a throne that brings on misery by its decrees" (v. 20).

The psalm has three parts. In verses 1–7, the unnamed psalmist calls on *God the avenger*. He asks God to judge the wicked. These arrogant evildoers prey upon the most helpless in society, like the widow, the foreigner, and the fatherless (v. 6). We've seen throughout the psalms that such terms, while they express the social and economic condition of people, are also symbols for God's faithful and oppressed people. The wicked "crush *your* people; they oppress *your* inheritance" (v. 5, emphasis added).

In verses 8 to 15, the psalmist describes *God as the teacher*. The wicked are fools. One commentator translates "senseless ones" (v. 8) as "you stupid ones". These wicked people don't deny that there is a God in heaven but, in their arrogance, they believe that the God who made us is somehow blind and deaf to all we do and think (vv. 9–11). How foolish! God not only sees and hears what we do, He also blesses those who learn from His law and accept His discipline when they wander from it (v. 12). In Hebrews 12:6, we are told that "the Lord disciplines the one he loves" (see also Proverbs 3:11–12). Like the righteous of Psalm 94, the readers of Hebrews, too, suffered under cruel and unjust rulers. **Both Hebrews and Psalm 94 remind us that the Lord will protect us and use these sufferings for our spiritual good.**

In verses 16–23, the psalmist looks to *God the protector*. When the psalmist feels he couldn't endure anymore hardship, God's "unfailing love" (v. 18) and consolation keep him persevering. More than that, they fill him with joy. In the end, he is confident that the God of justice will "destroy them for their wickedness" (v. 23).

Paul tells us in Romans 13:1–6 that governing authorities are God's servants, appointed to bring about justice and order. But in our fallen world, there are governing authorities that promote evil and oppress the church. In Revelation 6, John sees all those who've been martyred because of "the word of God and the testimony they had maintained" (v. 9). They, too, like the righteous in Psalm 94, are crying out to God for vengeance, "How long . . . until you judge the inhabitants of the earth

and avenge our blood?" (v. 10). The Lord's word
of comfort to them is "to wait a little longer"(v. 11).
One day soon, God will answer the cries of the
psalmist and the martyrs. "Amen. Come, Lord
Jesus" (Revelation 22:20).

How have you
experienced the
loving discipline
of the Lord? What
spiritual lessons did
you learn?

In the light of Psalms
93 and 94, how can
we pray for those
whom God has
appointed to rule
over us?

Day 45

Read Psalm 95

I once heard a church deacon said, while leading the holy communion, that there are two great motivations for obeying God: fear and love. Then he added, "But the Bible prefers love". Certainly, we love because He first loved us (1 John 4:19), but we mustn't underestimate or be apologetic for the motivating power of fear. Fear saves lives. In my country, there are warning signs at beaches that say, "Beware of sharks" or "Beware of crocodiles". If we ignore these warnings, we might die. Proverbs tells us that the fear of the Lord is the beginning of wisdom (Proverbs 9:10), and the lack of fear of God is the pathway to folly and destruction (Proverbs 1:32). The apostle Paul similarly admonishes believers to have a proper fear of the Lord (2 Corinthians 5:11, Philippians 2:12).

Psalm 95 begins as an exuberant song of joy to the Lord. The psalmist calls us to sing to the Lord, firstly, because He made all things (Psalm 95:3–5). Everything belongs to God, from the highest mountain peak to the deepest ocean valley, and everything in between. But there is another reason to "bow down in worship" (v. 6): the Creator is also the Shepherd of His people (v. 7). He provides all we need for life, and He guides and protects us.

We have a wonderful, powerful, and loving God. How could anyone turn away from Him? The sad reality is: it happens. Hence, in verse 8, the psalm takes a surprising turn from worship to warning. The psalmist reminds his readers of the great rebellion of their ancestors. After being saved from Egypt, Israel grumbled about the lack of water in the wilderness (Exodus 17). God heard their cry but the place is called "Massah (means testing) and Meribah (means quarrelling) because the Israelites quarrelled and because they tested the Lord" (v. 7). Later they rejected the Lord and wanted to return to Egypt. Then the Lord said, "not one of them will see the land I promised" (Numbers 14:23). The psalmist warns his generation—and us—not to make the same tragic mistake and fail to enter God's rest.

In the book of Hebrews, the author made a similar warning to Christians who, like Israel in the wilderness, are being tempted to turn away from Christ and return to their old life. Repeatedly, he warns them and quotes Psalm 95. Hebrews 4:1 exhorts, "Let us be careful". **In Christ, we have the wonderful hope of eternal life. This is our true rest. But we must be careful not to turn away from Christ.**

Recently, a local paper told the story of a pastor who had lost his faith. It made it sound like he'd lost his car keys. Psalm 95 describes such rebellion as the hardening of heart (Psalm 95:8). Many who call themselves Christians have allowed their hearts to go astray (v. 10). So, let us not be too quick to dismiss this warning as not applicable to us. The Lord is saying two things to us today. First, worship God and rejoice in Him. Second, fear God and "make every effort to enter that rest" (Hebrews 4:11).

ThinkThrough

Read Numbers 13:1–14:4. What was it that caused Israel to rebel against the Lord? Do we face the same temptations and challenges? How can we take heed of the warning today?

In our life and our Christian teachings, what place should there be for warning people about the consequences of unbelief?

Day 46

Read Psalm 96

Some Christians are critical of modern Christian songs. Their complaints are mostly the same: these songs are empty of any content, or they're too repetitive. These faithful saints would be happy just to sing the old hymns. I sympathise with their complaints, but Psalm 96 begins, "Sing to the LORD a *new* song" (v. 1, emphasis added). It would be a great loss if we were to stop singing the wonderful songs Christians have sung down the centuries. But we need to continually write and sing new songs too. We need to continue to write songs in the language and musical styles of today. And sometimes a new situation, like a celebration or a tragedy, might be better expressed in the words of a new song. I thank God for the contemporary songwriters who bless the modern church with their new compositions.

The first three verses provide the foundation for the psalm. First, "all the earth" (v. 1) is commanded to sing to the Lord. This isn't just all people but all created things (vv. 11–13). **God deserves praise from the billionaire and the baker, as well as the badger and the banyan tree, for He made them all.** And the songs we sing should "proclaim his salvation" (v. 2). While there is a place to just sing God's praises, good songs remind us of how God has saved us, especially in the death and resurrection of our Lord Jesus Christ.

There is only one God. All other gods are either pieces of wood or stone (v. 5) or fictions of the human imagination. The psalmist heaps up words of honour to God, whom he ascribes splendour, majesty, strength, and glory (vv. 6–8).

Psalm 96 commands all people to fear the Lord and tremble before Him (vv. 4, 9). Perfect love drives out fear (1 John 4:18) and Christians don't live in terror of our loving heavenly Father. At the same time, as we saw in Psalm 95, we never want to presume upon our salvation and live carelessly. Rather, we must "work out [our] salvation with fear and trembling" (Philippians 2:12). Psalm 96 reminds us that there will be a judgment day for every person (vv. 10, 13). While the Lord Jesus has taken our sins away, "we must all appear before the judgment seat of Christ" (2 Corinthians 5:10). This should evoke godly fear in the hearts of us all.

The psalmist instructs all creation to rejoice because God comes to judge the world (Psalm 96:13). In the book of Revelation, the heavenly hosts and the believers who have died in

Christ are heard worshipping God. Like Psalm 96, they pile up words to describe His greatness (Revelation 5:12). They sing songs of salvation, worshipping the Lamb (vv. 9–10). They also rejoice in God's judgment (19:1–5). Perhaps the greatest lack in the modern church is that we don't often hear this call. Announce and sing, "he will judge the peoples with equity" (Psalm 96:10).

This is a psalm to be sung more than studied. Take a few moments to "worship the LORD in the splendour of his holiness" (Psalm 96:9).

Why do you think the singers of the Bible see the coming judgment as an event for joy and praise, while the modern church prefers to ignore it?

Day 47

Read Psalm 97

Why should Christians sing to God? There are many reasons. Songs teach us wonderful truths about God and salvation. Songs help us to remember. Try putting a Bible verse to music and you'll find yourself remembering it better. Psychologists tell us that singing is good for our emotional health. When we sing together, we express our unity as God's people. But there is another important reason to sing: God tells us to do so! From the first verse ("let the distant shores rejoice") to the last ("praise his holy name"), we are called to be glad, rejoice, worship, and praise.

Verses 1–5 paints a glorious and terrifying picture of the God who is worthy of all praise. The psalmist uses imageries that remind us of Israel's days in the wilderness, where God shows His presence by the cloud and pillar of fire (Exodus 13:21). The cloud both reveals and hides God. When the cloud came, Israel knew that God was in her midst. But this cloud hid God from them, protecting "the people from a lethal dose of God's glory" (Tremper Longman III, *Exodus*). The fire symbolises God's judgment on His enemies (Psalm 97:3). Besides cloud and fire, the psalmist also uses lightning to describe God's frightening presence. At Mount Sinai, Israel experienced God in the lightning and thunder and "everyone in the camp trembled" (Exodus 19:16). So awesome is God's presence that even mountains, symbols of immovable strength, "melt like wax before the LORD" (Psalm 97:5).

Repeatedly we have seen in the psalms that one expression of God's glory is His judgment on the wicked. Promoting righteousness and justice through salvation and judgment, is so central to God and His work that the psalmist portrays them as "the foundation of his throne" (v. 2).

In verses 6–9, the psalmist calls on all things to worship God, from the heavens above and all peoples on earth (v. 6), to the false gods and spiritual powers that lie behind them (v. 7; see 1 Corinthians 10:19–20), to his own people in the villages of Judah (v. 8).

The psalm closes by addressing the righteous (v. 11), the faithful followers of the Lord. He exhorts us to hate evil (v. 10). 1 John reminds us, "if anyone loves the world, love for the Father is not in them" (1 John 2:15).

Finally, the psalmist rejoices in God's blessings on His people: He guards and protects them (Psalm 97:10); He shines His light on them, driving out darkness and fear; He fills their hearts with joy (v. 11). The only appropriate response is to say "rejoice in the LORD, you who are righteous" (v. 12).

A non-singing Christian or church is a contradiction. Certainly, there's more to praise and worship than singing songs, but it is not less than that. To be a Christian is to sing.

Why do you think some Christians don't like to sing in church? How can we encourage our non-singers to appreciate singing?

Reflect on the terms used to describe God's people in Psalm 97:10–12: "those who love the LORD", "faithful ones", "upright in heart", "righteous". What do these expressions tell you about the character of a Christian?

Day 48

Read Psalm 98

In Psalm 98, God has thrown a party and everyone and everything is invited. Parties are happy occasions in celebration of a special event like an anniversary. Psalm 98 is a thoroughly joyful celebration of God's salvation.

Once again, the psalmist invites us to sing a new song (Psalm 98:1). Commentators speculate that this psalm was written after the Lord gave Israel victory on the battlefield. However, the psalmist doesn't give us any historical context. Rather, he just rejoices in God's salvation. This suggests that any saved person in any place and at any time can sing this song.

The gospel is "the power of God that brings salvation" (Romans 1:16). It was on the cross that God's "right hand and his holy arm" (Psalm 98:1) worked salvation for His people. It was on the cross that God shows that He "remembered his love and faithfulness to Israel" (v. 3), and kept His promise to save His people by forgiving their sins. The priest, Zechariah, proclaimed this when, in celebrating the coming of the Messiah, he sang how God "has come to his people and redeemed them . . . as he said through his holy prophets of long ago" (Luke 1:68–70).

Since God is king over all the earth and His salvation stretches to the ends of the earth, then "all the earth" are to join in joyful praise to God (Psalm 98:4–6). It is not just people who are to lift their voices to God, the psalm invites the seas, the world, the rivers, the mountains, and all the creatures who inhabit these places to join the choir in praise of God (vv. 7–8). The Bible often personifies creation. In Psalm 19:1, the psalmist wrote that "the heavens declare the glory of God". He portrays creation as a preacher delivering a powerful daily sermon. Jesus said, even "the stones will cry out" at the coming of the king into his city (Luke 19:40). Paul portrayed the creation as a pregnant woman "groaning as in the pains of childbirth" waiting for the coming glory (Romans 8:22). God made all things, and each and everything, in its own way, is to give Him glory.

All over the world people sing in different ways. In some cultures and churches, the congregation stands still and people's faces don't show much emotion. In others, the people love to sing out loud, shout, and dance. Of course, what's important is the inner attitude more than the outward expression. However, it's striking how exuberant Psalm 98 is, "Shout for joy . . . burst into jubilant song . . . with trumpets and the blast of the ram's horn" (vv. 4–6).

Singing in the temple must sometimes have been very noisy. **So, whatever our cultural expression, knowing God's salvation is worth singing about with great joy.**

ThinkThrough

Look again at Psalm 98:1–3. In light of the greater salvation God has won for us in the Lord Jesus, what is the new song that we sing as Christians?

The psalms contain songs of lament and songs of praise. What principles can we draw from the psalms for singing in our churches?

Day 49

Read Psalm 99

Today there are 26 monarchies that rule over 43 countries. These rulers include kings, queens, sultans, emperors, and emirs. Some of these kings exercise real power, while others just serve a ceremonial function. Most of the countries in our world, to varying degrees, are democracies. In theory, a democratic nation is run by the people themselves, through their elected representatives. But who really rules?

Psalm 99 proclaims that God reigns. The psalm says three things about the divine king. First, He is the *universal* king (vv. 1–3). One of the paradoxes of Christian truth is that God is everywhere, but He especially lives amongst His chosen people. The psalm begins by calling on all the nations to tremble with fear because God is their king. Immediately the focus shifts from all the nations to one nation, Israel, where "The LORD sits enthroned between the cherubim" (v. 1). The cherubim on the ark of the covenant, located in the Holy of Holies in the temple, is another way of describing God's presence amongst His people. Verse 2 expresses the same dual truth, "Great is the LORD in Zion; he is exalted *over all the nations*" (emphasis added). Therefore, everyone should praise God's great and awesome name (v. 3).

Second, He is the *just* king (vv. 4–5). A king's responsibility is to rule justly; the people's responsibility is to honour and obey their ruler. When the King of kings comes to live amongst His people, He brings with Him justice and equity, or fairness (v. 4). His people, then, show these qualities both in how they treat each other and the people around them. These displays of the righteous character of God should lead all people to "exalt the LORD our God" and "worship at his footstool" (v. 5). The footstool was also a feature of the ark of the covenant in the Holy of Holies, adding to the image of the nations coming to Zion to worship God.

Thirdly, this awesome king is our *personal* king (vv. 6–9). **The God of Israel and the church is a listening and a speaking God.** The Bible records over 3,000 times that God speaks. In this section, we see three of Israel's leaders who called on God and heard God speak to them (v. 6). Our personal God is also worthy of praise because He forgives and judges (v. 8).

There is one other great affirmation about God in this psalm, one that sums up all of God's wonderful attributes: He is "holy" (vv. 3, 5, 9).

It's a word expressing that there is no-one and nothing like Him in power, love, justice, compassion, patience, wisdom, and goodness. The only appropriate response to the God of Psalm 99 is to "exalt the LORD" (v. 9).

ThinkThrough

God rules the world and God rules the church. In what ways is God's rule over the nations the same as God's rule over His people? In what ways are they different?

What do you learn from this psalm about what it means to have a personal relationship with God?

Day 50

Read Psalm 100

I have spent much of my working life teaching in Bible colleges. It's been a wonderful privilege. Sadly though, some students testify that the years spent studying the Bible and the wonderful truths about God were spiritually dry. As their minds were filled with knowledge, their hearts grew colder towards Jesus. They found it hard to pray and to sing joyfully. Something is seriously wrong when growth in knowledge about God doesn't produce hearts that are filled with more joy and thanksgiving to God.

Psalm 100 is an enthusiastic psalm of praise. It's a psalm in two parts that both make the same point. **The foundation of praise is knowledge, and true knowledge of God should lead to the right worship of God.**

The psalm begins with a three-fold invitation to praise God: "shout for joy" (v. 1), "worship the LORD" (v. 2), and "come before him with joyful songs" (v. 2). Why does God deserve our praise? Verse 3 gives us three reasons. First, He is our Creator. We'd have no life apart from Him. Second, we are His people. He is our Redeemer. He made us His own by purchasing us with the blood of His Son (1 Peter 1:18–19). Third, He is our Shepherd, who feeds, protects, and guides us.

The second part of the psalm (Psalm 100:4–5) repeats this important truth that the true knowledge of God leads to true praise. Again, there is the repeated call to thanksgiving and praise (v. 4). Verse 5 begins with the important word, "For". Once again, we're given three reasons for praise. Our thanksgiving is based on our knowledge of the character of God. He is good. He is loving. He is faithful. All of these wonderful truths were perfectly made known to us when God became man in the Lord Jesus.

There are two important things to learn from this psalm. First, any worship of God that isn't based on a true knowledge of God is empty and shallow. Jesus said, "God is spirit, and his worshippers must worship in the Spirit *and in truth*" (John 4:24, emphasis added). Any worship not based on true knowledge does not honour and glorify our great God and Saviour.

Second, the purpose of the knowledge of God is that it leads to true and joyful worship of God. There is no spiritual value in simply reading and studying more and more about God and the Bible if it doesn't transform our hearts and lives. If the only thing this short book on Psalms has done for you is to help you better

understand the Psalms, then it has failed in its main purpose. Having journeyed through Psalms 50 to 100, I pray that we have developed a greater love for God and others.

In your study of God and the Bible, how can you guard against it becoming spiritually dry and not life-transforming?

How do we ensure that the singing in our churches is based on the true knowledge of God?

Going Deeper
in Your Walk
with Christ

Whether you're a new Christian or have been a Christian for a while, it's worth taking a journey through the Bible, book by book, to gain a deeper appreciation of who Jesus is and how we can follow Him.

Let faithful Bible teachers be your tour guides and help you draw closer to Christ as you spend time reading and reflecting on His Word.

JourneyThrough
Psalms 1–50
Mike Raiter

JourneyThrough
Proverbs
David Cook

JourneyThrough
Ecclesiastes
Philip E. Satterthwaite

JourneyThrough
Hebrews
Robert M. Solomon

JourneyThrough
Galatians
Khan Hui Neon

JourneyThrough
1 Peter
David Burge

JourneyThrough
2 Peter & Jude
Eileen Poh

Journey Through with your
Bible study group!

Many of our *Journey Through* books now come with group Bible study lessons. All our lessons include printable handouts and lesson plans, which are free for you to use. And several have video contributions as well. Why not *Journey Through* with your Bible study group at **ourdailybread.org/studies**

Browse and purchase all our available *Journey Through* Series books at **ourdailybreadpublishing.org.uk/journey-through**

For information on our resources, visit **ourdailybread.org**. Alternatively, please contact the office nearest you from the list below, or go to **ourdailybread.org/locations** for the complete list of offices.

BELARUS
Our Daily Bread Ministries
PO Box 82, Minsk, Belarus 220107
belarus@odb.org • (375-17) 2854657; (375-29) 9168799

GERMANY
Our Daily Bread Ministries e.V.
Schulstraße 42, 79540 Lörrach
deutsch@odb.org • +49 (0) 7621 9511135

IRELAND
Our Daily Bread Ministries
64 Baggot Street Lower, Dublin 2, D02 XC62
ireland@odb.org • +353 (0) 1676 7315

RUSSIA
MISSION Our Daily Bread
PO Box "Our Daily Bread",
str.Vokzalnaya 2, Smolensk, Russia 214961
russia@odb.org • 8(4812)660849; +7(951)7028049

UKRAINE
Christian Mission Our Daily Bread
PO Box 533, Kiev, Ukraine 01004
ukraine@odb.org • +380964407374; +380632112446

UNITED KINGDOM (Europe Regional Office)
Our Daily Bread Ministries
PO Box 1, Millhead, Carnforth, LA5 9ES
europe@odb.org • +44 (0)15395 64149

ourdailybread.org

Sign up to *Journey Through*

We would love to support you with the *Journey Through* series! Please be aware we can only provide one copy of each future *Journey Through* book per reader (previous books from the series are available to purchase).

If you know of other people who would be interested in this series, we can send you introductory *Journey Through* booklets to pass onto them (which include details on how they can easily sign up for the books themselves).

☐ **I would like to regularly receive the *Journey Through* series**

☐ **Please send me ____ copies of the *Journey Through* introductory booklet**

Just complete and return this sign up form to us at:

Our Daily Bread Ministries, PO Box 1, Millhead, Carnforth, LA5 9ES, United Kingdom

Here at Our Daily Bread Ministries we take your privacy seriously. We will only use this personal information to manage your account, and regularly provide you with *Journey Through* series books and offers of other resources, four ministry update letters each year, and occasional additional mailings with news that's relevant to you. We will also send you ministry updates and details of Our Daily Bread Publishing products by email if you agree to this. In order to do this we share your details with our UK-based mailing house and Our Daily Bread Ministries in the US. We do not sell or share personal information with anyone for marketing purposes.

Please do not complete and sign this form for anyone but yourself. You do not need to complete this form if you already receive regular copies of *Journey Through* from us.

Full Name (Mr/Mrs/Miss/Ms): _____

Address: _____

_____

Postcode: _____ Tel: _____

Email: _____
☐ I would like to receive email updates and details of Our Daily Bread Publishing products.

Signature: _____

All our resources, including *Journey Through*, are available without cost. Many people, making even the smallest of donations, enable Our Daily Bread Ministries to reach others with the life-changing wisdom of the Bible. We are not funded or endowed by any group or denomination.